Foreword

THROUGHOUT life you will come across experiences to which there seems to be no answers. Not in this earthly lifetime, anyway. These experiences leave a deep impression within us, as we strive to understand. In this book the author tells of several such experiences he has had as a young policeman and in his private life. The author, Brian F. Smith, is my brother and what prompted him to write this book was the transformation of our brother Rockney.

Rocky was a very special person. He loved everyone and all who knew him loved him. He had a way of getting through to people without ever speaking a word. He was born severely handicapped and unable to take care of himself in anyway. His whole life he was cared for by his family who loved him dearly. As we, his siblings, stood by his bedside, just a couple of days before his death, the most amazing thing took place. We watched in wonder as his features gradually changed. We could not help but comment on the changes taking place. Our eyes were transfixed on him. We could not pull them away. Although we saw these changes occurring, we could not actually see any part of his body move. His body altered from that of a 61 year old man to that of a little Comment [BS]: boy. He was perfect in every way. His features then gradually reverted to the way they were before. What we were seeing was impossible, yet it was happening right before our eyes. It was the most amazing and beautiful thing I have ever seen!

As you read these stories you ask the question, "Why?" But the answer does not come. Everything must happen for a reason. We don't know the reason but hopefully one day we will. Brian has tried many sources looking for answers but all to no avail. In this book he tells of his own theories.

Please read this book with an open mind. There will be those who will find some of the contents hard to believe and had I not seen Rocky's transformation with my own eyes I may have been one of them. But I did see it and I am left wondering, We really must believe that one day we'll understand!

Margaret Freitag.

Why?

Tell me what is normal
Who is to say?
Everyone is normal
In a special way.

Everyone is equal
Our feelings are the same
Perhaps we cannot let you know-
Tell me, who's to blame?

It isn't fair, we did no wrong
Why must we live this way?
Are we being punished?
Perhaps we'll know one day.

I cannot bathe nor dress myself;
I cannot walk alone;
I cannot make my own decisions
But I have a loving home.

This was written by my twin sister
Who knows what my thoughts would be
If only I had the privilege
Of being intellectually, free.

Barbara Andrews.
(Written in honour of my much-loved twin brother).

Close to the Brink

THE stench of rotting nutrients and animal fats together with old soapsuds and bubbling ammonia gas must have been overwhelmingly putrid, yet, at the same time, curiously attractive to an extremely young and growing mind.

It happened quite suddenly really. One minute I was peering down into this thick grey revolting mass of froth and bubbles, not unlike the water in my mother's copper every Monday after she had finished boiling all the family's clothes that we had worn over the past week. Except that, this was murkier! Much murkier! And it smelt different.

The smell from the water she discarded from the copper was thick and humid, more like the air you inhale when stepping out of an air-conditioned aeroplane straight into the heavy humid sticky air of the tropics, although, I had not experienced such, at this time in my life.

This smell was like a magnet drawing me closer. A magnetism like that in tales told by New Guinea natives of how crocodiles would lay for hours on the banks of a river with their mouths wide open allowing their putrid breath to flow from their throats and drift freely on the passing breeze. This smell would attract any unfortunate passing dog and compel the poor instinct prone animal to investigate its source, and, often lead the curious canine to its earlier than otherwise, demise.

On this occasion, I too was similarly mystified. As I got closer my interest intensified. It gave me an intimate, threatening, yet at the same time cosy feeling, but most of all, it was undoubtedly irresistibly intriguing. These bubbles were of all sizes, quite frothy, with pieces of soap and food particles clearly visible through their otherwise opaque spheres.

The next minute I found myself suddenly breaking through this cloudy surface only to witness an even murkier subsurface. Pieces of floating debris floated past my eyes and I found I couldn't breathe. It was quite warm really. Almost comfortable! Something was telling me to get out of there quickly but do what I may, I couldn't return to where I had come. I was very alone and utterly unable to change my circumstance. What else was there to do but close my eyes and sleep?

Now! The point of all this is that I don't recall seeing any bright light at the time. Nor do I recall any long past relatives standing there waiting patiently with outstretched arms and a welcoming smile on their rather ghostly faces.

An experience such as my own near drowning would normally disappear into a person's sub-conscious and be unlikely to re-surface again throughout an entire lifetime. However, one must wonder at times how much in the sub-conscious of the past determines our inner most thoughts today. Do these thoughts of otherwise seemingly long forgotten experiences, continue to help shape our varying attitudes to certain aspects of life, as the journey of life itself moves on? Or more importantly, nears its ending.

The truth is that I was musing over these events when trying to imagine what it would be like to finally pass on from this life, and that was the closest I had ever managed to get to experience such an event occurring on my own personal level.

However, that would have undoubtedly been the end of it for me if it was not for the vigilance of my elder brother, Max, who ran to my mother with the news, "Mum, come quick, Brian has fallen into the gully trap!"

When my terrified mother unceremoniously dragged me from the stinking cesspit a few minutes later I was blue and not breathing. A doctor, who was hurriedly summoned to the scene, soon had things under control and I continued with my life without any further dramas of that magnitude.

I would have been too young to remember the precise details of my early childhood near drowning in my parents' gully trap. In fact, I hadn't thought about it all my life, until now! My clear visions of what happened on that day must surely have come from family recounts of the event handed down over the years, not from my own inner most thoughts. But I honestly can't remember my family ever talking about that occasion. At least not in any detail. We have never gone into the matter in depth, at least no one did with me personally. In addition, Max my eldest brother, died from an epileptic fit when he was about sixteen while I was no more than five or six. He therefore did not have the opportunity of playing the elder sibling role of hero. If it were not for his quick action and keeping a cool head on that rather fateful day, I would have been no more. However, it was not Max who reinforced these memories. Who but myself, and myself alone, could possibly harbour such an intimate memory?

Rockney, my younger brother, was a twin brother to my sister Barbara but while Barbara was born quite healthy, Rockney was born with Downs Syndrome. Although not understood at the time, doctors treating him in his later years believed he could also have suffered a stroke at birth, an affliction that left him completely helpless and quite backward for the rest of his life, never to speak a word, nor feed himself, nor carry out his own personal care at any level.

Max never got to spend a lot of time with the twins, although he was only 14 at the time of their birth, he tragically died two years later. But the time he did have with them was time he cherished. He loved them dearly and was not often away from them during those two short years.

Rockney had to fight for this meagre life he was born to live, however inadequate it may have been. At one point when he was still a baby our mother thought he was dying from a respiratory illness and after quickly arranging to leave us kids, Max, Margaret, Barbara and myself with a close friend, caught a Melbourne suburban train at Bonbeach for a rush trip to the Royal Children's Hospital in the centre of the city itself. When no more than halfway there Rockney ceased moving. He also appeared to stop breathing which left our mother alone on the train believing with all her heart that she had lost him. Our, by now silently frantic mother, had to leave the train at the Flinders Street Railway Station, the main city railway terminal at that time, and catch a tram in Elizabeth Street through the city proper to the hospital, with what she believed was her dead baby son in her arms.

Doctors at the hospital managed to revive him however and he lived on. Our father was at work in another part the same city while this episode was being played out, totally unaware of the trauma his wife was experiencing not far from where he was busily toiling in his trade as a French Polisher. Rocky and I now shared a common and close bond. Both of us came close to the brink and both of us survived – but Rocky was to pay dearly for his survival.

The Ghost on the Road

ROCKY, despite being appallingly disabled enjoyed much affection. All family members sincerely loved him. As we all grew and went to school, Rocky remained a baby. He required hand feeding, he wore a nappy, and he crawled around the floor on his bottom.

Despite all this, he had a distinct personality of his own, he had a mischievous sense of humour and he showed no respect for British Royalty, as all other British citizens of Australia during the 1940' and 50's had to, since we were foremost British subjects and members of the almighty British Empire of the day. Rock didn't know it but he dared to be rebellious.

Queen Victoria, (it is claimed) once decreed that it was not proper for bare legs to be publicly viewable. She is supposed to have ordered that ladies dresses were to be worn to ankle length and it naturally followed that as tables had legs they too were to have tablecloths draped over them. Everybody in those days placed long flowing tablecloths over dinner tables so that table legs also remained hidden from view.

This Royal decree, if such a decree was actually ever made, apparently annoyed Rock and he was not shy in showing his contempt for it.

A regular 'trick' of Rocky's, if placed close enough to the dining room table, was to reach out as quick as lightening, grab the table cloth and pull it out from under whatever utensils happened to be placed upon it. He would then roar with laughter. The closer to meal time the better, as more items placed on the table would create greater havoc among those present. Everything placed on the table would go flying in all directions. We siblings would also find much merriment in such behaviour for none of us would dare be so brave.

We had an aluminium teapot. It had been one of mum's favourites and it remained so despite its many altercations with Rocky that left it considerably dented. Whenever Rock was within distance that old aluminium teapot went flying – full, empty, hot, or cold. Its landings in diverse parts of the kitchen invariably ended in Rocky breaking out in uncontrollable laughter. Often, if it had occasioned a special landing of some manner, for instance, if it had brought something else down with it, like a cup and saucer or plate, he would remember the incident throughout the remainder of the evening. He would invariably break out into open laughter, after a short period of giggling and shaking with impending merriment, as his memory worked overtime recalling the details of the earlier event. Everything else was reasonably safe, as it was the table cloth and teapot that were his main targets, pretty well throughout his life.

I am sure these highlights of Rocky's life encouraged him to walk. He would sit for hours 'eyeing off' his quarry. Often giggling with the thought of what he could do if he could just get to either his beloved table cloth or teapot in some way. We all made sure they were always placed out of his reach until one day he just got up out of his chair and took a couple of wobbly steps. We were all thrilled with his achievement but it was not to be long before those steps facilitated him getting from his chair to his target. Neither the table cloth nor teapot could be adequately protected from that day on.

As we siblings grew, married, began raising our own families and building our own careers, there was always one of us who didn't, and that was Rockney. Rock was always home and wherever Rock was, that's where home was.

During my own youth I pursued my own career path quite differently to the life my brother was destined to live, and, as a young man, late one night, I found myself driving an Australian Army bus along the Point Nepean Highway in Victoria. Being the early hours of the morning meant the highway was quieter than usual. The passengers were asleep readying themselves for the next working day except for myself and maybe one or two other soldiers. We hadn't seen another vehicle travelling in either direction for over 20 minutes now and we were nearing our destination, the School of Signals Balcombe Army camp.

We were travelling at around 100 kilometres an hour quite comfortably.

Being a highway, the carriageway was wide and the bends were well banked and long. Now and again a side road entered the main road and now and again there was a cross road but all these roads had a stop sign facing them which gave us the 'right-of-way' all the way through. Vision was clear and despite the early hours I was quite wide awake and enjoying the traffic free driving conditions.

I was a driver in the Australian Regular Army Signals Corps and the previous afternoon I had received orders to drive a team of Army basketballers to a basketball match in one of the Melbourne suburbs. This was a weekly occurrence during this time of the year as it was mid-basketball season.

The driver allocated this job each week was given the day off before coming on duty at about 6 pm so he could get a bit of sleep in beforehand. It was known from experience that by the time the game ended and the players socialised with the other team for a while it was always at least the early hours of the morning before we arrived back in barracks. The driver, of course, could not drink alcohol at the celebrations that followed each game. Doing so was a chargeable offence.

We had all been to the game and had been on the road for at least an hour. The earlier revelling and a few songs, which usually followed a victory, had died down, and all was quiet inside the bus.

Looking out ahead to where the white centre line appeared to merge into the blackness of the night at the end of the headlight beam, I thought I could see something in the middle of the road. I could not quite make out what it was but I began slowing the vehicle down as I approached by taking my right foot off the accelerator pedal. As I got closer the 'object' appeared to be straddling the white centre line so I lightly touched the foot brake to slow the bus even more. I soon realised the 'object' was indeed a person standing in the middle of the road looking in my direction. I pressed the foot brake pedal even further thinking that something must be wrong and I had best be ready to stop. I soon realised the person I was looking at was actually coming at me of his own volition and I would have to brake even harder to avoid a collision. I braked hard and pulled the steering wheel firmly to the left but the person I was focused on at this stage kept on coming at me. It became frighteningly obvious that I was not to avoid colliding with this person whom I couldn't get away from no matter what I did. When the point of collision became obviously inevitable, we hit, and the man on the road thudded into the windscreen with his face pressed hard up against the glass, level with mine. All I could see was his abnormally pale face with terrified looking larger than normal eyes, staring through the glass directly into my eyes. I couldn't believe what I was seeing. His face hit the windscreen.

I pulled over onto the gravel on the shoulder of the road and stopped with a sudden jolt. I was considerably shaken and I felt the blood drain from my face.

"What the bloody hell's going on Smithy?" I heard a voice call out from the back of the bus amid a few, 'shit', and 'bloody silly bastard,' exclamations before everything went quiet, obviously waiting for an explanation for their sudden jolt back into consciousness.

"I've just ran over a bloke!' I explained as I raised myself from my seat to go outside. You could hear a pin drop inside. Everyone was stunned till someone said quite loudly.

"Hell Smithy are you serious?"

I was the first to alight but it was not long before everyone in the bus was outside with me. I went to the front of the vehicle but there was nobody there. Someone handed me a torch but I couldn't see any marks. No blood, no hair, no scratches anywhere, not like what I expected to see. Some of the soldiers looked under the bus while others walked back along the road but to no avail. No body was to be seen and no sign of any collision existed.

"You bloody well went to sleep Smith, you've been dreaming!" some voice said with apparent agreement from most, if not all of his colleagues, including myself.

"Do you reckon you're right to drive?" someone enquired.

Although still feeling a bit shaken I assured them that I was fit to drive on and we all piled back on board for the remainder of the trip, this time with everybody wide awake.

No more than two or three minutes later, we came to a rather blind turn in the road. Old large pine trees lined either side of the highway and the headlights shone directly into these big bushy trees causing a restricted view of the highway appearing before us as we rounded the bend to the left. As the lights pulled around to the left the full road ahead became visible again only to show the whole roadway was blocked before us. A large semi-trailer was across the road at right angles to the road itself. The cabin of the truck was resting in a storm water drain constructed alongside the side of the road. Upside down beside the truck was a horse drawn fully laden milk cart. Broken milk bottles were all over the road and it appeared the horse, lying motionless on its side, on the roadway, was dead.

We were the first on the scene and we all piled out once again, for the second time that night in no more than a few minutes, to see if we could be of any help. We found the driver of the semi-trailer, still seated behind the steering wheel of his truck, staring vacantly into space. He was obviously in shock but appeared to be physically intact. The driver of the milk cart was lying motionless near the centre of the road, on his back, between the horse's legs. He appeared to have an abnormally pale face, blood draining from his mouth, and ears, his large lifeless eyes looked terrified. He looked as if he had not moved after being catapulted there by the collision. I felt certain he was dead.

A nearby resident who heard the crash had notified the authorities, and it was not long before police and ambulance officers arrived at the scene and took over.

The truck driver told police that the milk cart had entered the highway from a side road. By the time he recognised what was happening, it was too late to avoid a collision despite him desperately pulling his vehicle across the road and into the ditch. The truck's trailer swept out across the path of the horse and cart overturning it, with considerable damage resulting.

We all quickly realised that if we had not stopped the other side of that bend we too would have been part of the fatal accident, ploughing into the whole mess at somewhere near 100 kilometres an hour.

Suddenly my visionary apparition changed, in my passenger's minds, from a sleepy hallucination to a clear warning that imminent danger lay ahead.

The story went around camp for quite a long time claiming the vision on the bus windscreen that night had been none other than the driver of the milk cart himself not wanting any further catastrophe to occur that extraordinarily fateful night. I never challenged this assumption.

A Waste of a Life

DRIVING around a large city at night can be an exhilarating experience. There is always something happening as people continue darting from one place to another for God knows what reason, some doing good some doing evil. Some are at work, like street sweepers, cleaners, taxi drivers, restaurant staff, entertainers, doctors and nurses, prostitutes and police officers. The list goes on. Many are just passing the time away. Others barely exist, living a solitary life with intolerable personal loneliness.

A thriving city keeps many from their sleep, as they, especially the young, do not want to miss a minute of city life at night. The lonely find they are unable, for one reason or another, to participate in the joviality experienced by many other young lives out there enjoying themselves. Their loneliness deepens and for these people a city can be cruel and heartless. To them there is no one to talk to, everyone else appears too busy either in recreation, or in working, and after a while, they find themselves being ignored and being left completely alone.

Police officers often run across such people, usually when it is too late to do much for them. Busy city nightlife workers and revellers from time to time pause to consider that something is not quite right with someone they have temporarily crossed paths with and inform the police of their concern. It then falls on the police to investigate what inevitably turns out to be another unfortunate human tragedy in the midst of so much spontaneous gaiety and life.

I experienced one such occasion first hand when I was a young 22 year old Victorian police officer. My term of enlistment in the Army had been completed and I had joined the Victoria Police Force. I was stationed at the main Melbourne central police station in Russell Street and on this particular night I was driving a police divisional van, known affectionately as a 'paddy wagon'. I was a constable and my colleague in the van with me was a senior constable.

Whilst patrolling the streets on this particular night shift we received a call over the police two-way radio system known as 'D24'. We were told we were required to attend at the Victoria Coffee Palace in the tree lined 'Paris' end of Collins Street.

The Victoria Coffee Palace was a well known multi-story boarding house. It was one of the cheapest such places in the city and therefore was home to many young people, usually from the bush, who were away from their family home, some for the first time, trying to make their own way in the 'big smoke.'

We attended the call immediately and soon found ourselves being ushered along a dimly lit, second story narrow passage with a dark, highly polished, wooden floor, centred upon which was a long, narrow length of old, well worn carpet, to soften the noise of people walking on the otherwise bare boards. There were dark brown stained wooden doors every three or four metres with little black numbers implanted on a white ceramic disc about head high, leading into little one bed, cell like rooms.

The night shift manager of the hotel, who was leading our small procession, stopped outside room number 105 and pulled a set of master keys from his pocket. He inserted one of the keys into the lock and turned it. We could all clearly hear the click as the lock opened. He then turned the door handle and pushed but the door would not budge. The senior constable and I tried to assist him by adding our weight but the door still refused to budge.

"Something is stopping the door from being opened from the other side," the night manager wisely observed, stating the obvious.

The senior constable looked at the situation for a while then said to me, "You're pretty skinny Smithy, come here and climb up onto my back and see if you can squeeze yourself through that little window at the top of the door."

He then bent over to make it easier for me to clamber up onto his back and when I was ready he slowly straightened. This allowed me to reach the window but as the glass was frosted, I could not see through. I fiddled around with it for a while and felt it move. It wasn't locked! Moreover, with a bit of wrangling I managed to pull it toward me far enough to allow me to look through. I observed that a large wooden wardrobe had been moved until it completely blocked the doorway, jamming it tight, but it allowed me to crawl through the window, which was, luckily above the wardrobe's height.

A single incandescence light bulb hanging from a cord in the centre of the small room was still burning albeit on low wattage. It was not bright as I could clearly make out the filament fusing without having to turn my eyes away. I then focused on a young girl sitting up in her old-fashioned cream painted iron framed single bed with a light cream bedspread, covering her legs. She looked as if she was peacefully reading a magazine, totally ignoring me approaching her from above the wardrobe. She had the magazine in her hands and it was open. The pages held firmly between her fingers.

Looking around the tiny room, I noticed a fully drawn dull brown coloured blind hiding a small single window opposite the blocked door. There were no curtains. The room, painted a light musty green colour, looked as if it was well overdue for another coat.

I jumped down from the top of the wardrobe onto the floor, making a loud thumping sound and went over to the motionless girl. I touched her arm, she felt quite cold and clammy. I had never touched a dead human being before but I felt certain that I had on this particular occasion. Her eyes were closed and she appeared quite pretty, with long straight fair hair. "No more than 18 or 19 years of age." I thought to myself. I then went back to the wardrobe and dragged it away from the door to let the other two men in. The senior constable went straight to the girl in the bed then asked the night manager to call an ambulance immediately.

Now alone in the room with me, the senior constable asked me to shut the door and to list everything in my notebook exactly where it lay. The most noticeable items were three empty tablet bottles with no lids on them, lying on their sides on the top of a small wood stained bedside table; their lids were lying alongside them. A sheath of writing paper containing handwritten notes lay with them. I picked up the notes and started reading. It soon became obvious to me that it was a suicide note. The first I had ever read. The writing started out being quite well written but as it neared its ending it started wandering off the page. I could still make out the final words, "I'm feeling very sleepy now and I must finish. I love you mum and dad."

The letter explained that she came from a large Victorian country town and was dearly missing her family. It indicated she was a trainee nurse working at one of Melbourne's main hospitals and was finding it hard to make new friends. She said she was upset by the fact that a boy she had befriended in Melbourne was not, and would not be accepted by her family. He came from the same town as she, but 'from the other side of the tracks.' He had been raised in a state housing department estate, the son of quite poor parents, and she was the daughter of a prominent shopkeeper.

They were known to each other, growing up in the same town, and the lad had come to Melbourne to play football for one of the Victorian Football League sides about the same time she left town to study nursing. He also felt alone in the big city and they had formed a firm friendship, brought together because of their common hometown links. And common city loneliness.

She went on to say the matron at the hospital, who was apparently in charge of her teaching, was very hard on her until it had finally got her down. "I can't take it any more," she said. She went on to blame the matron for being the 'straw that broke the camel's back.' Her letter expressed a deep feeling of helplessness. She said she felt she could not meet the expectations of her family nor that of her matron at the hospital, she felt she could not meet their exacting standards and that her life appeared, to her, to be worthless. The letter spent some time expressing her sorrow for letting her family down and she asked for understanding. She went out of her way many times to express her deep love for her family as well as for her boyfriend as her handwriting became harder and harder to read.

I told the senior constable what I had found and handed it to him. He read it then handed it back.

"O.K Smithy," he said, "You know what to do, this one's yours, ask me if you need any help."

With that said, I was left with compiling a report for the coroner, having the body identified and notifying her parents.

We waited till the ambulance arrived to take her to a hospital doctor where she was officially declared dead, before we removed everything from the room that had been hers, being very careful to tag every item including the suicide note.

I had the Shepparton Police notify her parents personally and the next morning accompanied them to the City Morgue where they formally identified her as their daughter, before I handed them all her personal belongings that would not be required should an inquest into her death be opened.

They, naturally, were devastated. It was a very sad occasion. A young person who had her whole life before her saw no way out of her personal predicament at the time. If her life could have been saved she most likely would have been a mother and grandmother by now and her life could well have helped many others and have proved to be very worthy.

However, it was not to be. Why did she have to die? A young life! A healthy body!

Why was she allowed to die while others fight desperately to live on in crippled bodies? All we do know is that on her last lonely night in Melbourne she decided to end it all in a dingy, cheap hotel room, alone, whilst outside her covered window the city continued with its shameless unknowing haste full of life, vitality, and... loneliness.

Her 'spirit'? We can only assume it parted from her body quietly to traverse whatever pathway nature had prepared for it on such occasions.

Too Young to Die

I WAS on day shift in the Melbourne inner suburb of Carlton undertaking foot patrol of the area alone. Carlton had, during the late 1800's, been a centre of much underworld activity. It had been a working class suburb housing workers who worked in the heavy industries of Melbourne at the height of the industrial age. As a result much of the suburb became slum areas consisting of little one and two bedroom shantys. Today it is considered more ' middle class' but there are still pockets of working class high rise government apartments. Especially on its north eastern fringes.

It had been a quiet shift so far with nothing happening apart from handing out a couple of parking infringements and an obscured number plate booking. The kind of offences you concentrated on simply to keep boredom away on such uneventful shifts.

Without warning, I suddenly heard a quite loud screech of rubber on bitumen followed by a sickening thud. I had only heard such a sound once before and that was when doing my police training at the Police Depot adjacent to the Prince Henry Hospital on St Kilda Road.

Our squad, 11 Squad of 1962, was on the parade ground undertaking drill training when our attention was drawn to a woman standing on a rail on the seventh floor balcony, in full view and directly opposite where we were on parade. She was wearing a pink coloured nightgown that reached to her ankles and was hanging on to a balcony support with her right hand. Without any sound or warning, she suddenly let herself fall over the side of the building. On the way down one of her outstretched arms hit a lower balcony rail thereby emitting a loud crack like sound as it broke. A sound similar to that of a point 22 rifle discharging. This sound was followed soon after, by a dull, heavy sickening thud as her body hit the pavement. We found out later that she had been a cancer patient at the hospital negatively reacting to information regarding her prognosis.

I was hearing the same heavy sickening thud sound again this particular afternoon. I instantly recognised it.

Fearing the worst, I looked to where this most recent sound appeared to have come from and saw a group of people collecting in the centre of the road near a stationary bus no more that 30 or 40 metres from where I was standing. A car was stationary in the middle of the road where a group of bystanders was forming. As I neared the scene, I heard a woman start to scream from the direction of the multi-storey State Housing Department flats opposite. After forcing my way through the throng of onlookers, I saw a girl of no more than, nine or ten years of age, with long flowing blonde hair lying prostate on the roadway near the front of the large metropolitan bus parked at a bus stop. There was a late model Holden car stationary in the middle of the road forward of the bus and facing the motionless child. I knelt down besides her and checked for a pulse, first on her wrist and then her neck. I felt nothing. At this moment, the woman whom I had heard scream from the direction of the flats had reached the scene.

Still screaming uncontrollably, she forced her way in to where I was bent over the child. She was horribly distraught and, totally ignoring my presence, pulled the girl up into her arms. Her screaming grew louder and tears were streaming down her face.

I tried, without any success whatsoever to console her mental anguish, for she was uncontrollably panic stricken at the time and I knew that I had to free the child from her grasp. Although I believed the little girl was dead, I could not be sure. She may well have been in need of immediate resuscitation. She may have had a broken back. I did not have the answer to these questions. I finally freed the girl from the woman as gently as I could under the circumstances and some bystanders took her to the side and hugged her. By this time, an ambulance and police assistance was heard approaching and it was not long before the girl was receiving expert attention from the paramedics.

One of the ambulance officers said to me, "I suppose you already know that she is dead." I nodded knowingly.

The ambulance officers then placed the lifeless little body in the back of the ambulance and drove off after giving me their names and where they were taking her. The police from the Accident Appreciation Squad began measuring up the scene and I focused my attention on the hysterical woman, whom after a while, I talked into taking me back to her flat where we could talk about what had just happened.

Along with some of her friends, we entered the concrete slab construction and walked up a narrow, cold stairway. I had my arm around the woman, who was in her late twenties, as we continued up the stairway, until we got to the third floor. I tried to keep her in conversation fearing that she would go into shock as she was sobbing heavily.

One of her friends, who was leading the way, took us through an open door and into one of the flats. It was a small two-bedroom unit but it appeared homely and warm. It had many family pictures hanging on the wall. Photos of the woman with a taller dark haired man, whom I assumed was her husband, and the little girl, were everywhere. There were no pictures of other children. I took this to mean the girl was an only child. I noticed that the kitchen window overlooked the scene at the bus stop.

Some neighbours made us a cup of tea while I explained to her in the softest way possible that her beautiful daughter had died. There is no easy way to impart such news to a grieving parent, who not only does not want to hear it but is also mentally refusing to accept it. Except that, it must be persevered with in the best and most humane way possible. I finally managed to quieten her down. She then told me that she had given her daughter some money to go across the road to buy some milk at the corner store opposite the flats where they lived. She said she had watched her run across the road from the kitchen window and as soon as she heard the screech of the tyres and the following thud, she knew instantly what had happened.

I had a friend of hers call a doctor and got a message to her husband to return home from work immediately. When satisfied all had been taken care of I left her in the care of her friends whilst I, still on foot patrol, caught a tram into the city where I met some people at the City Morgue who had earlier told me they were willing to identify the child formally.

After that duty was performed, I caught a tram back to the Carlton Police Station to complete a report for the Coroner. On arrival at the Police Station, the driver of the car that had hit the girl was still patiently waiting for me to give me a written statement.

He, a minister of religion by occupation, told me in his statement that he had pulled out to pass the bus that was stationary at a bus stop. When drawing level with the front of the bus a small girl ran out in front of him. He said he had braked immediately, as hard as he could, but could not avoid hitting her. Other witnesses also testified to a similar story and nobody claimed that the minister had been travelling too fast for the conditions. It appeared that nobody was to blame. It was purely coincidental, or accidental. Her mother asked her to go to the shop for her to buy some milk at the same time as a large bus pulled into a bus stop to drop off and pick up passengers. The bus's presence at the bus stop prevented the driver of the car seeing the girl run out onto the road until it was too late to stop and the bus's presence prevented the girl from seeing the car coming that she ran in front of.

***

Little was I to know at that time, six years later, almost to the day, when stationed at Morwell as a First Constable, my wife Shirley and I had to endure a similar experience when we lost our second eldest child, Gregory.

It was early morning and I was still in bed when I heard Shirley scream from Gregory's bedroom.

"Brian, come quick Gregory's dead!" she screamed. I immediately went to her side where she was peering into the cot where three-month-old Gregory lie. She had a horrified look in her eyes. I looked in the cot where she had moments before pulled the bedclothes back only to see the lower side of the baby's head was a dark blue colour, the upper side was quite white.

I took her out of the room and sat her down at the kitchen table then rang the Morwell Police Station informing the duty sergeant of what had occurred.

The pain we both felt that morning was devastating. My thoughts went back to that quiet day in Carlton where I consoled the grieving mother of the little girl fatally hit by the car driven by the minister. It was very hard to think clearly but we still had two other children in the house who needed protection from the overbearing grief we were feeling, David our eldest and Brian Craige whom we had adopted whilst stationed at Fawkner before coming to Morwell.

Gregory had been dead most of the night, probably soon after he had been put to bed after his last bottle at around midnight. He had died of a little understood syndrome known at that time as 'Cot Death', more latterly known as Sudden Infant Death Syndrome, or SIDS. No real reason is given for such tragedies, they just occur, and humankind appears unable to prevent them.

Surely, life must be at its greatest value in its youth, when one's whole future is still waiting to be experienced. I began wondering, as once again there was no sign of any spirit presence to help ease the pain on either of these tragic occasions. The feeling of loss was enormous.

***

Morwell itself is a major Victorian country industrial centre adjacent to the massive Yallourn coal deposits with a cosmopolitan mix in its population. It is also situated on a major highway, the Princes Highway that links Melbourne to Sydney via the east coast of south east Australia and it is surrounded by massive coal fired electricity power stations feeding power to the city of Melbourne some 150 kilometres to its west.

It was an ideal area for a young police officer to gain valuable experience in a wide area of policing.

I undertook my share of the heavy workload but for some inexplicable reason I was jinxed with experiencing well above my share of violent deaths. At one stage, I was in the process of completing no less that seven briefs for the coroner in just one week. The deaths ranged from a woman and two of her children who died when a car they were travelling in, driven by her drunken husband, hit a bridge railing on the outskirts of the town. The force of the impact ripped her arm from her shoulder, leaving her lying on the roadway and her left arm about two metres away in her full view. She was still conscious at this stage and asked me to place her arm in the ambulance with her before being taken away to the Traralgon Hospital. She died on arrival at the hospital. One of her sons, about seven years of age, died instantly at the scene whilst his elder brother about nine appeared uninjured but died of internal haemorrhage on the way to the hospital. I recall wrapping the lad up in my uniform great coat because he was complaining of feeling intensely cold. The drunken father escaped injury, he didn't suffer a single scratch.

Another horrific accident that same week involved three young party goers seated in the front seat of a utility vehicle that ran off the road at a very high speed. As the vehicle left the roadway it began cart wheeling therefore throwing all three occupants from the vehicle, two through the front windscreen and another through the passenger side door.

I was the first on the scene and became aware that something was wrong when I noticed car headlight burning about 50 metres from the roadway, in a paddock and up against a solitary tree. When I stopped to investigate I first ran across a girl of about 18 years who had been thrown through a barbed wire fence at high speed. The force of impact broke the wire that subsequently wrapped itself around her body causing horrible incisions from her neck to her thighs. She was conscious when I reached her. Conscious enough to ask me to unwrap her from the wire entangling her body. I did so but she died during the process.

I then left her and kept walking towards the car that still had the headlights burning. On the way I ran across another girl lying in the grass. She was unconscious. I then noticed a male nearer the vehicle. He was unconscious also. By this time, another police car had arrived to assist me, along with two ambulances. I had earlier notified the police station by two-way radio that it appeared I would need back up, before leaving my own vehicle to inspect the scene. The first girl I had attended was indeed dead, as I had suspected. The second girl I had encounted died later in hospital. The male survived although he was destined to spend the rest of his life as a paraplegic.

These three young people were in the prime of their lives. They had been to a party in nearby Churchill and had left temporarily to return to Morwell. They were returning to the party when the accident occurred.

A further fatal accident I attended that week occurred at the end of a quiet night shift. I was finalising my paperwork and getting ready to 'knock off' as soon as my early morning replacement arrived, when the station phone rang.

It was from a farmer's wife who lived about 10 kilometres out of town. The woman who was speaking on the other end said that a tractor had rolled over onto her husband and she could not free him. I rang the local ambulance station then left the office immediately, for the farm.

On arrival, the wife and two of their young children took me to the scene. With her help, we lifted the tractor high enough to place a block of wood under it to stabilise the machine sufficiently to gently pull the unfortunate man free.

He was not breathing and I could hear the ambulance in the distance. I decided we could not wait any longer and I had best begin resuscitation there and then. I blew into his mouth then began pressing my palms against his chest. My hands went further into his chest than expected and blood pumped out of his mouth, nose, and ears. His ribs had apparently broken when his tractor had earlier rolled onto him. If he had not died then he was certainly not living now. I handed him over to the ambulance officers and apologised prolifically to his family. It was a young family. A family that had, up to now, relied heavily on the presence of the now deceased farmer for their very existence. All their lives changed that day.

**

Some argue that it is fate. I was finding that hard to believe but I was desperately looking for some reason.

What possible 'fate' based reason could explain the deaths of young people enjoying each other's company in a party atmosphere?

What possible reason could explain the loss of a mother and two of her children in such horrific circumstances?

What possible reason could explain the deaths of innocent babies? None! There was no reaching out from the 'spirit world' and all those affected had to deal with their individual situations purely on an earthly basis. Fate means by implication that each life has a blueprint that determines one's future and that nothing can alter its course.

If this were to be accepted then the young girl who died alone, from her own hand, in her tiny bedroom at the Victoria Coffee Palace would also be a victim of fate!

My thoughts went out to my younger brother Rockney and I who were both granted another go at life in our formative years, but for what reason, when no mercy at all was being shown to others who by all accounts were equally innocent of any transgression. Rocky was still living with my mother and father. Rockney's life had not changed all that much since I had left home to pursue a life of my own with my own family.

He was still being hand fed and his walking ability remained limited. He retained a strong fixation with tablecloths and aluminium teapots, neither of which was safe if he be left alone with them as he would either hurl the teapot or pull the tablecloth out from under anything that may be set upon it.

Home with Rock was now at Mildura in Victoria. My parents had moved there with Rockney's twin sister Barbara and younger sister Lynette.

When they first moved to northern Victoria, where the summer temperature often reaches 40 degrees Celsius, Rocky found it hard to become acclimatised. Air conditioning was only in its infancy and quite expensive. Mum had to hang wet hessian at the front and back doorways of the house in an attempt to lower the temperature of the air as it drifted inside from the intense outside sunlight, to extend to him the best relief that she could.

Once the sun went down the intense heat gave way to countless mosquitoes that swarmed on any patch of exposed skin.

Both mum and Rock took life one day at a time. Tomorrow held no fear for either of them for whatever it held they felt helpless to make any changes.

My mother fully accepted her fate. Rocky didn't know the difference.

Craige

I FIRST met Craige when he was no more than 10 months of age. He appeared to have been somewhat neglected. Pus-laden sores were plentiful on his young body, and he was both unhealthily overweight and dirty. His outstanding features were his plentiful curly red hair and accompanying freckles on his innocent little face.

I had been working alone, on night shift, at the Fawkner police station when I received an early morning phone call.

"Could you come out to Elsa Street?" the caller asked, "we have a baby here that the mother has deserted."

It was eerily coincidental that I had received such a call at that time as Shirley and I had been married for what we considered to be, 'some time', much the same as my mother and father before us, after they were first married, and we too were concerned that we had not become parents at this point in time. We had consulted various specialists in that field of endeavour but were constantly being told that there was nothing physically stopping us from having children of our own. It was however quite frustrating, especially after Shirley suffered an early miscarriage.

I drove out to the address given, a typical Melbourne working class area, consisting mostly of recently built three bedroom brick veneer houses, in a still developing housing sub-division that was representative of the fast growing northern suburbs of the day. As I pulled up outside the address that had been given me I noticed a light burning in a front room of an otherwise darkened house.

A woman who appeared to be in her late thirties to early forties, with a complexion that indicated she had experienced many hard times in her life and who spoke with a rough voice, seemingly to vindicate my earlier observations, met me at the front door.

She told me that an acquaintance of hers had left a male baby with her telling her that she did not want anything more to do with him. She added that she was not in a position to take on the responsibility of bringing the baby up herself and wanted to rid herself of him also.

As it was the early hours of the morning, it was not appropriate to call out the police women, who would normally have handled such a situation, so I bundled the little fellow up, along with all his worldly possession that consisted mainly of a pram, bedding, and a small amount of clothing, and took him to my own home.

Shirley was asleep at the time, so I woke her.

"Do you still want a baby?" I asked her as she sleepily responded, quite mystified by my question at that early hour, and compounded by the fact that she was quite aware that I was still on duty.

I quickly explained the situation to her and took her outside to introduce her to my new friend who, by this time, was sound asleep in his pram on the back seat of the police car. She soon warmed to what was being offered and gently carried the little fellow inside with her, with myself not far behind carrying his meagre possession. I then returned to work.

Later that morning when I returned home after my shift had finished, a completely different looking child greeted me. Shirley had spent some time bathing him and removing the pus from his sores. He looked clean, fresh, and happy. I had compiled a report for the policewomen regarding the situation and mentioned therein that my wife would be happy to care for the child until the mother was located rather than have him placed into foster care at that early stage.

His biological mother was, in due course, found to be living in Sydney but reiterated that she still did not want anything to do with the child.

Shirley and I had become accustomed to having the little fellow around by this time; we therefore began the process of legally adopting him. His biological mother was more than happy to oblige and it transpired that we eventually did adopt him as our own.

Soon after we welcomed Craige into our family group, Shirley became pregnant with David and not long after that Gregory was born.

Craige brought a lot of happiness into our lives despite the devastation we encountered as a family group when Gregory tragically died of SIDS soon after his birth. It takes time to blunt the wounds created by the loss of a baby to a young couple and Craige, along with his brother David, through their youthful antics, helped soften these wounds. He grew up to be a fine young boy and eventually a fine young man.

When he was about 16 years of age, he had his palm read by a mysterious woman, Mrs Nicholson, who lived in the small bush village of Lachlan in southern Tasmania. We were living in nearby New Norfolk at the time. The woman and her husband John, a well-known local political identity, lived in the local church building. It was no longer operating as a church so they had purchased it and set it up as their home. She was a well-travelled woman who believed she had the ability to predict people's futures. Craige was a happy-go-lucky boy who thought this was to be a challenge for her so he offered up his palm.

"You will have a short life!" she told him, among the other usual utterances that are common to such people.

Craige was not perturbed about this prediction. I don't think he believed in it to any extent but every time we chastised him in anyway for his habit of living his life for the moment with no planning for his future he would always bring the matter up.

"I'm only going to have a short life," he used to come back at us, "so I may as well enjoy myself now."

He left school at the earliest opportunity and was plagued with not being able to secure any permanent employment so when the opportunity arrived for our family to move to Rosebery on the west coast of Tasmania he was overjoyed.

He obtained permanent employment with the local council immediately and became the popular coach of the local swimming club.

He was just 18 when he came home from football training one Thursday evening to announce proudly that he was to play in Rosebery's senior football side in the first game of the season.

Both he and David were good sportsmen and both were vying to be the first to play senior football. He was ecstatic that it was to be he, who was to be the first to obtain this distinction. Especially, because he was the elder of the two, and he felt it was fitting that this should be so.

When the Saturday morning of this important senior football game against Queenstown, at the famous Queenstown gravel oval, arrived, I was busy doing nothing special. Craige asked me if I'd drive him to the game, I declined telling him that I would be along later in the day but would enjoy a beer with him when the game was over.

He replied that that was "OK", so I wished him well with his debut, as he left the house to go to the local post office in the main street to get a lift with another player, John Sweeney, who was to play in the earlier reserves game.

It was not a long wait before John arrived to pick him up. As he had already picked up another player, David Pettit, who was sitting in the front passenger seat, Craige happily let himself into the back seat, immediately behind the driver.

The three young men then left Rosebery for the 60 odd kilometre drive to Queenstown. Both John and Craige were single at the time but David was married with a young family. The drive was uneventful until they reached an area known as Melba Flats about 25 kilometres into the trip.

Melba Flats is a well-known area owing to it being the rail head for ore trains carting copper from the Queenstown copper mine to the port city of Burnie 150 kilometres to its north. It is heavily wooded and at the foot of the range of hills between there and Rosebery that is full of blind bends and dangerous hill crests.

Just as the three young footballers entered the last cutting before the flat terrain of Melba Flats itself, they encountered a large truck looming over the crest coming directly at them on their side of the two-way highway. This truck was passing another truck filling its own lane travelling in the same direction. To their left was the solid embankment of the cutting. There was no way out and they must have instantly realised their dire situation.

Almost as soon as the predicament facing them would have been realised the truck coming at them hit them head on completely demolishing their relatively inferior vehicle.

Their vehicle, now reduced to a tangled mess of twisted metal, still contained their fit, youthful, but now badly damaged bodies. The truck driver, who was returning to Ulverstone, a coastal town to the north, after completing yet another one of his daily early morning milk deliveries to west coast towns, was uninjured.

Teammates who were travelling to the same game were shocked when they came upon the scene soon after the impact and quickly organised police and ambulance officers from Zeehan and Rosebery to attend. Soon after their arrival, ambulance officers lifted Craige from the back of the vehicle and laid him out on the ground behind one of their vehicles when two nuns who happened to be passing by stopped and spent some time comforting him despite him being unconscious.

It was about ten o'clock in the morning when the local police sergeant, Sergeant Davis, knocked on the back door of our house to inform Shirley and I of the accident in which Craige had been involved. He told us that if we attended the Rosebery Hospital it would not be too long before the ambulances brought the injured in for treatment.

I immediately went down to the local football ground, where another football match was taking place, that Craige's siblings, Matthew, Jamie and Cindy-Anne, were attending, to take them to the hospital with us to await Craige's arrival. David was attending Elizabeth College in Hobart and residing at the college's boarding house. Luke was a two month old infant.

It was not a long wait before the three young men, all fighting for their lives, arrived at the hospital. A Catholic priest who was driving through Rosebery at the same time heard of the accident on his car radio and dropped in at the hospital to see if he could be of any assistance. We, Craige's family members, were waiting anxiously in the hospital foyer with family members of the other two young men while the lone doctor, Dr Kulinski, worked frantically to save their lives. David Pettit died first.

Sergeant Davis requested an air ambulance be sent urgently to transport the two remaining men to a bigger hospital for treatment but was told only one air ambulance existed and that could only carry one stretcher case at a time. Therefore, one would have to remain. The doctor and the police sergeant were left with the choice, which of the two men would be left behind? To most likely die. The priest was with Craige when he died in mid-afternoon before the arrival of the helicopter therefore releasing the doctor and police sergeant of their onerous decision.

John Sweeney was ultimately air lifted by the air ambulance to a major hospital where he received appropriate treatment and survived.

Although not Catholics by religion, the local priest dropped by our house later to speak with our children who were finding the loss of their elder brother hard to come to terms with. The church also offered its services for Craige's funeral and following burial. A most unusual offer to people not brought up in their faith. We accepted the offer.

Over a decade later, my sister Barbara, who lived in Mildura, Victoria, at the time and her three daughters, Yvonne, Sharon, and Donna, decided to attend a travelling medium's show at the Mildura RSL Club.

During the course of the evening, the psychic, Luke Patrick, asked if anybody present knew of a young man who died following of a tragic motor vehicle accident involving three young footballers on their way to a football match. They were that stunned with the question they did not respond, instead they waited for further information, and not expecting such a subject so close to themselves to come up, were too nervous to speak up in such a public forum.

The psychic further explained that it appeared the young man trying to reach out to someone in the audience was going to play in his first major football game that day. They remained stunned and silent. After the session finished, whilst excitedly discussing the incident among each other, they all realised the significance and admonished themselves for not taking the matter further when given the chance. They rang me at the first opportunity with the information of what had transpired.

Upon my retirement from work soon after, Shirley and I made it a point of trying to track down the psychic involved. We were travelling around Australia in a motor home and got close to him on a couple of occasions but never actually had the opportunity of physically catching up with him, as he flew from venue to venue.

When we finally returned to Tasmania, we learned that he was coming to the island also and was to appear one night at the small east coast town of Triabunna, no more that 20 kilometres from where we were staying at 'Gumleaves' Little Swanport. We looked forward to the meeting with much anticipation but only a short while before the event was to take place I fell off a ladder and broke my right foot. One week prior to my discharge from the Royal Hobart Hospital, he left Tasmania for the mainland, and the meeting I had been yearning for, for so long, was once again beyond my reach.

A few years later Shirley and I had retired to Devonport on the North West Coast of Tasmania when we learned that the psychic Luke Patrick was returning to appear in Devonport at the local RSL club. Once again, our anticipation of gleaning more information regarding our much-loved son was heightened and we eagerly purchased tickets to attend with our daughter Cindy-Anne, who was now married.

I had never attended such an evening before and was unsure of what to expect. Mr Patrick introduced himself to the audience and got straight down to business. After a few encounters with various members of the audience he then asked:

"Is there anyone here who knows of, or had any connection with, a young girl who had been decapitated in a horrific murder/suicide case?"

Cindy sat up in her seat stunned!

"I have," she answered.

"She is trying to make contact," he replied.

After a short period of small talk with little being revealed, he announced that he was having trouble getting a message from the girl because a stronger presence was cutting in.

"It is the man who killed her. He is saying he is sorry."

Contact was lost soon after with little else learned.

Cindy's sister-in-law was decapitated in a particularly brutal murder by her former partner who later the same night hung himself out in the bush.

Craige never got a mention; perhaps he had successfully crossed over by now and had therefore moved on.

***

Our mother had died before both Rockney and Craige passed away. The burdens she carried almost all of her married life had finally caught up with her. She was exhausted and her heart finally gave way. On our mother's passing our father was unable to care for Rock so the task fell to his twin sister Barbara and his elder sister Margaret.

Barbara was living in Dandenong Victoria at the time with her husband Robert and their five children; Darryn, Yvonne, Sharon, Steven and Donna. Margaret's family were all living in the outback New South Wales township of

Wentworth, near the Victorian-New South Wales border.

Margaret, her husband Lothar and their family of Robert, Wayne, Warren, Keryn, Lynice, and Kelvin all lived in a small corrugated iron cottage on the banks of the Darling River.

Lynette assisted her two sisters from time to time when required.

All welcomed Rock into their midst where he received the same compassionate loving care as he had experienced all his life living with his mother and father.

His ability to care for himself had not changed and he remained totally reliant on others for his well being.

The Ouija board

BOUGAINVILLE Island, which is part of Papua New Guinea, is hot and humid. Heavy rains fall almost daily, usually mid afternoon, and the burning sun soaks the water up for the rest of the daylight hours, which makes the humidity even more severe ensuring a hot, heavy, sleepless night if you don't have the benefit of air conditioning. The same process is repeated the following day and again the next day, and so on. In short the weather becomes very boring as there are no distinct seasons as we know it, and take for granted, in southern Australia.

The people who are native to the island, are very dark skinned, 'skin all the same saucepan,' is how they describe themselves, referring of course the pitch black soot buildup on the bottom of a saucepan after countless use over an open fire. They are proud to be amongst one of the blackest races on Earth and they protect their women from us 'whites' and mainland New Guinea natives, who are much fairer than themselves, with large signs reading 'TABOO' in red capital letters outside most villages.

Taboo is pidgin meaning keep out and they mean it. To enter such a village you have to wait at its perimeter until somebody from the village comes out to enquire why you are there and then be invited in.

They are extremely superstitious and their culture is a world away from ours.

I was the officer in charge of security at the Loloho port site for the giant American construction company Bechtel-WKE who were building the massive open cut copper mine at Panguna in the centre of the Island in the early 1970's.

All equipment for the construction work had to enter the island via the Loloho port.

One of the first things you are told on starting work in Bougainville is not to stop at the scene of an accident. Whereas in Australia it is illegal to not stop at the scene of an accident, in New Guinea it is advisable to drive on.

The reason for this is their attitude towards death. An unconscious person in New Guinea is presumed dead and it is only God's will that allows them to awaken. This belief goes someway to explain the general acceptance of the deaths many youths who after being introduced to liquor such as whisky and rum for the first time, overindulge to the extent that they fall into a drunken stupor only to die in their sleep of alcohol poisoning. If a person is to die violently, like in a motor car accident or in an altercation of some nature, it is that persons 'wontok's' right, even responsibility, to see that retribution is accomplished. This means that a life can be taken for a life lost and it often is. The dead person's 'wontok' is a person who speaks the same dialect (one-talk). And as there are over 600 dialects in Papua New Guinea one has to be careful. We of course, being white and all speaking English, means that we are considered 'wontoks' of each other. This in turn means that if you run across an accident, one in which you are not involved in yourself but just want to help, you could well finish up in serious trouble. Especially if the driver of the hit run happened to be English speaking and, as a result of the collision, a person became unconscious. If the person was to miraculously regain consciousness again after your demise that would be God's will. It all tends to make you drive slowly and carefully at all times.

Even chooks and pigs are protected in this way, although not to the extent of taking a life for a dead chook. It will cost you, or your 'wontok,' a considerable sum of money or other kind of retribution to get out of the trouble you have caused.

Death is not taken lightly however. When one dies violently everybody is made aware of the situation immediately, no doubt to help watch each others backs would be one reason but there is also a sincere feeling of sorrow and regret. Their love for each other is profound.

On one such occasion whilst I was on Bougainville Island a worker found a dead body of a young man, lying face down on a large rock by the roadside between Loloho and Panguna, and it appeared one or more of the company's workers may have been involved. I was asked by the local police to help in the investigation. It was the morning of Christmas Day. I set up an interview area and had my men begin the process of interviewing our workforce one by one trying to ascertain where they were on Christmas Eve and who could vouch for their alibi. They all refused to cooperate in any way. It appeared the poor wretch who died was mentally challenged and they saw no wrong in his life being taken from him. Even his wontok's agreed with this belief and nobody was ever charged with his murder.

The youth in Papua New Guinea are very bright and easy to teach, mainly because they want to learn. Most of the indigenous workforce at the mine construction would have been under 25 and a big proportion of them in their middle to late teens. Massive big mining trucks with tyres alone higher than an average man standing upright were driven by teenage boys. Being young, these boys would often race each other back after unloading their overburden into the river.

The fast flowing river would wash thousands of tons of clay overburden a day out to sea, many, many, kilometres away to the east, destroying the livelihood of villagers living along the way. The company offered to rehouse these settlements in more appropriate areas away from the river but few, if any, took them up on it. Hence, a battle began between the old inhabitants of Bougainville and the international mining company Rio Tinto, who claimed mining rights over the underground copper that the construction workers were exposing, simply because they discovered it buried there. That was the main reason for my employment. To protect the company's property and assets from marauding locals who wanted all mining activity to cease.

One of these ore trucks overturned one afternoon whilst racing back to be reloaded and the driver was killed instantly after being thrown from the vehicle and crushed. The company passed the news of his death to his village on the New Guinea mainland, telling them that his body would be flown to them in a lead lined coffin and that on arrival at the airport they would be notified of its whereabouts. They could then retrieve it and transport it to his village for the funeral ceremony. This was duly arranged and his body was flown to his nearest airport where it was reported a message had been sent to his village for it to be picked up.

Two weeks later one of my native staff members came rushing into my office quite excited.

"Master, Master, you must do something, the boy we sent to his village has not arrived. Something is wrong!"

I asked how he knew this and he answered, "The Ouija Board told us master!"

Everybody seemed to use an Ouija Board for all sorts of reasons in New Guinea, even the police in solving crime.

"Don't be damned silly," I told him, "Its all been fixed up and finished now."

"No master, no!" he insisted.

Being a spiritualist sceptic at that time, with little tolerance for superstition, I told him to get back to work and put the matter out of his mind. A day or so later a small delegation approached me demanding I do something urgently about the boy's body.

"He is still at the airport master," they claimed. "He told us that nobody has been told to pick him up."

I thought I owed it to them to pass their concerns on.

It was not long afterwards that I received an apologetic message from the mine administration stating that there had been a foul up at the airport and the coffin did in fact remain there unclaimed. A further message had since been sent to the village rectifying the matter. My staff members were thrilled that I had listened to them.

As a result, I was invited, along with several of my Australian colleagues, to an Ouija Board evening with some of the indigenous staff. I did not take part but stood at the back of the room watching closely, with sceptical interest, everything that was happening. It was a reasonably small room and everybody seemed to be nervously smoking and drinking. The humidity was stifling. Cigarette smoke hung heavily in the air.

One of my fellow officers volunteered to take part and placed his fingers on the bottom of an upturned beer glass as instructed. The indigenous lad did likewise.

The glass started moving alarmingly. The indigenous boy quite abruptly, told the 'spirit' to 'go away'. He explained what was happening by telling us that some 'spirits' are trouble makers and can't be trusted. Things quietened down after that until someone very excitedly tried to make contact. It happened quite suddenly. A 'spirit' was trying to make contact by spelling out a message. It was doing this by moving the upturned glass to the appropriate letter of the alphabet that was printed on a cardboard sheet that the glass was resting on. In this manner it was slowly revealed that she was the officer's grandmother who had passed away some time beforehand. To prove her identity she spelt out her nickname that was only known within the family itself. He was close to shock. The communication went on with the gist of the message being that the officer's young son was fretting for his father, he had not spoken since his father had left home and as a result he had recently been admitted to hospital. The family were very concerned the woman's spirit told him.

The man was understandably disturbed with this revelation and immediately left the room to place an urgent phone call through to his home in far away Melbourne. His wife admitted on the phone that the boy was indeed fretting over his father's absence and was in hospital but she hadn't wanted to worry him about it. She said she thought the boy would ultimately get over it and they needed the extra money he was earning whilst at Bougainville. The father, who apparently enjoyed a very close relationship with his son applied forthwith to leave the island, for home. He flew out the following day.

***

My interest in the mysteries of the Ouija board was to become re-enforced many years later when the dangers of its misuse brought about a situation that cost an innocent young life.

It began among a small tight group of impressionable teenagers who all attended the same High School in Rosebery, western Tasmania. One of the most popular girls in the group had a young male friend who was in the workforce. He had a high profile among teenagers of the district because of his occupation as a local radio disc jockey and he invited her to a car ride from her hometown of Tullah to Queenstown some 60 kilometres distant. The invitation was particularly attractive because he was going to traverse the Anthony Road, which, although still under construction at the time by the Tasmanian Hydro Electricity Commission, was already being used by some inquisitive locals.

As the Anthony Road was a new road linking major dam construction projects for the production of hydro electricity to the Tasmanian electricity grid, nobody was yet completely comfortable with its navigation through some of the most mountainous areas of the island. The road was often wet from almost continuous drizzle and low cloud that formed heavy fog patches.

As the youthful couple neared the southern end of the road where it re-connects with the older Murchison Highway, the driver lost control negotiating one of the many tight curves. He smashed into an embankment on the opposite side of the road instantly killing his female passenger.

As news of her death found its way back to her friends they became increasingly depressed, unable to come to terms with the reality of the loss of one of their own under such circumstances, where, up until that time they had all youthfully believed they were invincible. They all had difficulty coming to terms with their loss and found comfort in the belief that she was actually still with them. If not physically, then definitely spiritually. They held séances almost nightly as well as regular usage of an Ouija board and on all occasions believed sincerely that they had found their friend who told them that she was now alright and enjoying her afterlife. On one occasion, some of her teenage friends were convinced that she 'appeared' to them in the local supermarket. On another occasion while using an Ouija board, they claimed to foretell a motor vehicle accident where an ambulance was required to treat the injured. It later turned out that an accident did occur at the location they specified and an ambulance was required to transport the injured.

All these stories added to their belief that their friend was still with them, albeit in spirit only, and that death was nothing to fear. Some even believed it could be an improvement on their present situation to such a degree that one young lad even suicided in order to share her experience with her.

"I want to be with her!" he told friends before shooting himself.

His death only intensified the supernatural activities of the young friends left behind and his grave at the local cemetery became the new focal point for more séances. The gloomy atmosphere these activities attracted eventually overwhelmed the entire town. Visitors to the village began commenting on becoming overwhelmed with an un-natural feeling of despondency when coming down the mountain before entering the town.

If travelling to Rosebery from the north you have to first climb and then descend Mount Black, the most heavily wooded rain forest in the planets southern hemisphere, to reach the picture postcard town of Rosebery, which nestles in a valley surrounded by wooded mountains, and divided into two by the ever flowing Stitt River. But first you have to traverse the flat country surrounding nearby Tullah and its trout filled lake, the reflective Lake Rosebery which mirrors the mighty eucalyptus growing profusely along its banks so well that it is difficult to determine what is real and what is reflection.

The majestic Mount Murchison towers over both Rosebery and Tullah much like a natural balustrade overlooking nature's wondrous work. On a sunny afternoon the shape of a large crucifix, that had formed many thousands of years ago, leaving cracks on the otherwise clear rock face, can be clearly seen high up on its northern rock-face. Further to the south stands Mount Read where the worlds oldest still living plant organism can be found, a 10,000 year old Huon Pine! Beneath the ground lays one of the worlds richest zinc lodes. It has been mined continuously for the last 100 years and it appears it will continue being mined for the next 200.

However, many of the young were obviously unhappy and sought solace in their paranormal activities despite being surrounded by so much natural beauty and its riches.

I found the eerie atmosphere intolerable and I feared for the mental health of the young if they failed to pull themselves out of their collective depression so I approached the local priest for his opinion. He was a tall thin man of Polish extraction of about 40 years of age with a rather dark complexion and a heavy accent. He listened patiently while I tried to explain my observations and I was relieved when he told me that he also felt something was wrong and that he felt it required some sort of spiritual intervention.

He later informed me that he had called on a South Australian priest to visit the town in order to exorcise the entire village. The mainland priest, who was contracted to perform the exorcism arrived soon after, he was coincidentally a former priest of the same parish and was familiar with the area. He completed the work he came to accomplish and left immediately after without talking to any of the teenagers involved. As soon as he left, the kids lost interest in their unhealthy obsession of the supernatural and they resumed their normal lives once again.

Rocky

ROCKNEY had three principal carers during his lifetime. His mother in the first instance and when she died he became his twin sister Barbara and his eldest sister Margaret's responsibility. His twin sister Barbara took on this role in conjunction with Margaret on a share basis for some time but this arrangement ultimately changed to Barbara caring for him full time after she moved into Mildura with her family. The youngest sister Lynette cared for him also from time to time, usually on a respite basis.

Despite Rocky's extreme backwardness in development both mentally and physically he possessed an ability to communicate, with his twin sister Barbara, certain happenings in their lives when they were apart. Many experts claim that the ability to partake in extra sensory perception, or ESP, as it is more commonly known, is restricted to identical twins only. Rockney and Barbara were not identical twins but they were twins having shared the one womb during their formative months within their mothers body.

When the twins were about ten years old Barbara experienced a bad fall at the Cockatoo Primary School in Victoria which she was attending. She slipped whilst jumping over some logs and hit her head. She explained later that she remembered seeing stars at the time and a severe headache developed instantly necessitating the school teacher, Mrs O'Leary, to place her in the sick bay for the remainder of the school day. At the same time that Barbara fell and hit her head their mother was feeding Rockney his lunch. She had him sitting back from the kitchen table when he suddenly threw himself off the chair and began screaming and holding his head for no apparent reason. Mum was so concerned that she asked his elder sister Margaret, who was home for lunch herself at the time, to take her bike and ride to a neighbours house where she knew there was a telephone and call for a doctor. Before Margaret got to her bike her mother called out for her to not worry as Rocky was now calm and had resumed eating his lunch again.

On another occasion, when adults, Barbara had to attend the Dental Hospital in Melbourne to have all her teeth removed because of decay. She had to stay in hospital overnight. Her husband Bob was home that evening looking after their children when he received a phone call from our mother asking him if everything was alright with Barbara, she explained that Rockney was moaning and rubbing his mouth for no obvious reason. He told her that Barbara had had her teeth removed and was still in hospital recovering.

It was during Barbara's period of care that Rockney developed the most. Much of this was due to her enrolling him with the Christie Centre in Mildura. The Christie Centre is a day care centre where mentally challenged people mix and are encouraged to involve themselves in a variety of basic life skill activities. They are taught to carry out various tasks suitable to their individual development capabilities.

Rocky's life skills were minimal as he had never before experienced any professional assistance such as the Christie Centre offered. It was here where he developed a certain sense of independence for the first time. It was here where he made new friends outside of his tight immediate family circle, in fact, he formed a very intimate, and close relationship, with a fellow Down's syndrome client of the centre named Maria, both their faces lit up every time they met. They obviously held deep feelings for each other. It became a very important time in his life. Rockney had never shown any real affection to anybody outside his own family circle before. He tended to shun strangers and he chose carefully who he got close to.

Rocky's experiences at the Christie Centre showed that he was capable of forming a relationship outside his own family as he obviously sought the company of Maria whenever he had the opportunity and he showed he enjoyed her presence. Maria was equally comfortable in Rocky's presence. Maria was not as physically handicapped as Rocky but she had limited speech which caused difficulty in her ability to make herself properly understood but just like Rocky she loved being with other people. Both had pleasant personalities. When Rocky entered the Christie Centre in the mornings Maria's face would light up with happiness. She would say his name and walk over to him with outstretched arms and embrace him. Rock always smiled back and it was obvious that he was equally pleased to see her. They often sat together with arms around each other watching the activities taking place around them. From time to time the centre would organise dance sessions for its clients and when this occurred Rocky and Maria would be seen 'dancing' together in their own style. It was obvious to everybody that they held strong feelings for each other. Soon after Rocky had to stop attending the Christie Centre because of his deteriorating health, Maria suffered a stroke. She was then placed in a nursing home. Barbara used to visit her on Rocky's behalf and was shocked to see her lying in her bed with her mouth wide open staring at the ceiling oblivious to anything taking place around her. On one visit Barbara took her a photo of her and Rocky together. In the photo Maria has the happiest of smiles and Rocky has his arm around her. Barbara held it up in front of her telling her it was her and Rocky. She actually turned her head and looked straight at it. Barbara left the photo with her and asked the staff if they could show it to her from time to time. Barbara also took Rocky to see her in his wheelchair but neither of them seemed to recognise each others presence. She died soon after.

The Christie Centre also introduced Rocky to horse riding. This was one activity that would have had his mother turning over in her grave if she was to learn about it. It was unthinkable that a person of Rocky's limitations could ever sit high up on the back of a horse without support. Let alone allow it to move under him. Throughout his life he had never shown interest in any kind of animal be it the more domesticated cats or dogs, let alone an animal the size of a fully grown horse. But it went ahead and Barbara was satisfactorily reassured when she went to visit him on his first attempt at this completely new experience. She was amazed to see Rocky sitting upright, as straight as a soldier and as proud as Punch, complete with his riding helmet, on top of a horse as it was led four or five times around the paddock with the proudest of riders on its back.

Under the helmet he wore the biggest and proudest grin that one could imagine. It was unfortunate that his introduction to horse riding came rather late in his life and he was not to enjoy it for long as he soon became too weak to sit upright anymore. His posture became quite hunched over and the enjoyment disappeared from his face. It was not long after he had to stop horse riding that he also had to stop attending the Christie Centre altogether.

Mildura, being sited on the Murray River, is the home of many house boats. The river is wide and slow running and is dammed at many locations by lochs to keep the river height at a constant level throughout the year. It is located in the hottest and driest part of Victoria and it is the river that gives the city its life. It was only a matter of time before the Christie Centre was to involve this most important lifeline the area possesses, with it clients, to help them enjoy its presence and understand its importance to an otherwise desert environment. Rocky received an invitation to attend a river cruise with other Christie Centre clients to enjoy a four nights and five days excursion to the neighbouring riverside town of Wentworth and back.

Wentworth is located on the New South Wales side of the river some 40 kilometres away as the crow flies but many times that via the winding river. It would be the first time that Rocky would have been away from any members of his family for so long. Permission was granted for him to go and it was not long before his adventure of a lifetime commenced. Once on board, the excited and happy clients of the Christie Centre with Rocky amongst them casually lied back and took in their new surroundings as their boat slowly meandered along the mighty river. They watched with widened eyes as they saw other people swimming and fishing and even water skiing, jet skiing or canoeing alongside. Evenings brought with it unparalleled stargazing opportunities without any city light pollution and complete silence as only outback Australia knows. During the daylight hours, beyond every turn there was a new surprise, as noisy galahs warned other birds of their approaching boat. Hovering hawks quickly silenced the noisy bush-life and it would not stir again until all signs of the hawk disappeared from sight. Now and again an inquisitive kangaroo stopped in its tracks besides an age old River Gum to take in the view of the touring Christie Centre personalities slowly passing by.

On their second afternoon on the river the happy group pulled in at Wentworth where relatives and friends of the passengers had been invited over to visit and spend part of the evening with them. Barbara remembers seeing Rocky on her arrival. He was sitting on a chair on the bank of the river watching a few of his friends trying to light a camp fire. He was intensely watching everything they were doing with an amused grin on his face. She said he was enjoying himself immensely with his friends.

Rocky loved music. He loved music playing in the background as it seemed to sooth him. When his attraction to music was discovered Barbara used to turn on the radio first thing every morning and it soon became her routine. One morning she went through her usual routine of showering him, feeding him breakfast then sitting him on the couch to await the Christie Centre bus. Rocky remained disturbed however, he was not his usual contented self. As Barbara sat him on the couch he growled at her in no uncertain terms. She could not see any obvious problems but he kept growling right up until the bus arrived. After putting him on the bus for the day and saying goodbye she returned to the house. The first thing she noticed was the silence. She had forgotten to turn on the radio.

Another routine was to take him to the toilet as soon as he got off the Christie Centre bus in the afternoon. When leaving the toilet he would growl at her in his own way if she tried to walk him in a direction other that where he wanted to go. Barbara always said that she loved it when he growled at her as it meant he had a mind of his own and was thinking for himself.

Routine even went as far as dressing. One morning, after showering, Barbara thought she was going through the same routine as usual in getting him dressed. But this morning he out-rightly refused to allow her to put his trousers on him. He actually pushed her hand away and moved his legs to one side. After a while Barbara realised that she hadn't put his underpants on. When she did he was quite happy to have his trousers put on. But it only happened the once. On other occasions she tried to trick him by purposely not putting his underpants on first before his trousers. But he had no idea what was happening. There was no reaction at all.

***

Rocky had another older brother beside myself, he was Max, and his entry into our family was important in itself for he became very close to Rocky when Rocky was a baby. Following the marriage of our parents in Tasmania in the late 1920's a period of discontent eventuated when they found that no children were forthcoming. Being eager to start a family they decided to foster a baby boy who was named Maxwell.

Max was a healthy and bright child and he gave them both much pleasure but whilst still a young boy he contracted meningitis and nearly died. On recovery however it was found that his brain had been damaged by the disease and he was subjected to regular epileptic fits. As a result he never attended school. Despite this considerable handicap he managed to become a close family member and helped his mother, to the best of his ability, in bringing up the other children who were to soon follow. First Margaret then myself and then the twins and later on Lynette.

I owe my life to Max as I have explained earlier in this writing as he used to watch over us all like a 'mother duck'. Not much would go on with Margaret and I without Max knowing about it. But it was the arrival of the twins that really brought about his 'maternal' instinct. He especially attached himself to the twins particularly Rocky who was unfortunately born far more disabled than he himself. Although very ill himself his main interest in life was in playing with the twins.

Max's affliction with epilepsy was worsening as he got older and he was a handful for our mother to handle with four other children, two of whom were only babies and one of them seriously handicapped and quite ill. When Max was sixteen he became quite weak and was suffering from regular seizures. He asked his mother if it would be alright if he played with the twins again when he got better. He never did, as he died soon after when recovering from a particularly bad Grand Mal seizure.

Our mother had been watching over him as he was fitting on this final occasion and when he had finally settled down she covered him whilst he was sleeping and came into the adjoining lounge room to sit with the rest of the family who were all assembled there together. It was not long before she exclaimed to our father.

"Frank, Max has just died."

"Don't be silly Hazel" dad replied.

"Yes, Frank," she insisted, "he has died, I just saw his spirit go up the stairs."

Our sister Lynette recalled her brother's life with the following words:

On the 11th of September 1943, Mum gave birth to a beautiful baby boy she and dad named Rockney. Only fifteen minutes before she had given birth to a beautiful baby girl who they decided to name Barbara. You could imagine their surprise when the doctors told her there was another baby there.
Mum and dad had no idea she was having twins! They were so happy! They had no idea how these births were to change their lives.
The doctor told Mum that Rock was a 'real little gentleman,' because he let the 'lady go first.'
Margaret and Brian were so excited to have a new brother and sister; they stood at the gate at the front of their home telling all passers-by the good news. A man walking past, on witnessing their excitement over such an event, gave them sixpence each. They immediately raced inside to tell their mother of their good fortune. Sixpence in those days was a considerable sum of money for children to have in their possession.
Mum had a feeling something was not right with Rock. He was eventually diagnosed as having Downs syndrome.
When the twins were about six weeks of age, Rockney suddenly

became ill with pneumonia. Dad was at work, so Mum organised a babysitter (a friend) to watch Max, Margaret, Brian, and Barbara while she took the train from our home in Bonbeach to the Royal Children's Hospital in Melbourne. During the journey, Rock, cradled in Mums arms, became worse and Mum really thought he had died. When she arrived at the hospital, the doctors were able to revive him, much to her relief.

Dad was working in Melbourne but mum was unable to let him know what had happened until he arrived home from work at the end of the day.

Mum and dad were later told they should not expect Rock to live past the age of sixteen, but if he did, he would live to be a man.

Doctors, at first, said he would eventually be able to walk and talk but on their last visit to his specialist, Dr Southby, he revealed that Rock was more backward than first thought. He said he still thought he may walk but doubted if he would ever talk.

A few years before Rock died, he needed a CAT scan, and it showed that at sometime in his life, possibly at birth, he had had a stroke. It was thought that this might have been the reason he was never able to talk.

We were all sitting in our lounge room when Rock was 10 years of age when he suddenly got up off the chair he had been sitting on and walked from one corner of the room to the other. He then undertook this new activity of his repeatedly. It was a very exciting time for all of us.

Mum and Margaret were so excited they went off to church and told their friends the exciting news. Rock did not walk again for another week, but after that, there was no stopping him.

Even though we all knew, Rock was not the 'same' as us we never looked on him as being any different. We treated him the same as we treated each other. He had a happy childhood.

Our father had a stone quarry at Cockatoo, a small Victorian country town, while we were all growing up. Dad, at times, placed a plank of wood across the quarry to facilitate easier access to the other side. One day Rock went missing, we all went looking for him and could not believe where we found him. Rock was almost half way across the quarry on the plank. It was no use calling out to him because we feared he would just get the giggles and fall, so Margaret walked across the plank and led him back by the hand.

It was unbelievable how he managed to keep his balance on the plank. Rocky had a great sense of humour throughout his life.

Mum always put a tablecloth on the table before we sat down to eat a meal. Rock had a 'thing' for the tablecloth and seemed to always wait until there was crockery placed on it, and then he would make his move. When satisfied nobody was watching he would make a beeline for the tablecloth and pull on the end of it so hard that everything placed on it would crash to the floor. He would then take off as if his life depended on it, laughing his head off. When Mum growled at him trying to chastise him for his action he would only laugh louder.

The teapot was also a favourite of his. Mum always left it standing by the side of the wood-fired stove but placed at the back and out of reach of Rockney. However, repeatedly and unexpectedly, he would somehow reach out and swipe it clear across the room. Once again, he would laugh his head off when he heard it crash to the floor. The teapot developed a reputation for its many dents that resulted from Rock's numerous fun filled games.

After a meal, if any food remained uneaten he would always pick it up and indiscriminately shove it into his mouth. He had to be watched with food because he could choke himself easily.

I can clearly remember when we lived at Sassafras in the Dandenong Ranges in Victoria. Barbara and I would sit on Rock's bed of a morning and play with him. He would be sitting up in bed rocking backward and forward and humming to himself. When he did this, we would grab hold of his chin and move it up and down. The sound he was humming would then appear to be saying 'mum'. We would call Mum into the room and tell her Rock was calling out her name.

He would often giggle and make funny sounds that appeared to be, 'da, da, da.' When this occurred, we would do the same again with his chin until it sounded as though he was saying, 'dad, dad, dad'. He thought all this was hysterically funny and would giggle like mad as a result. He would laugh that much his shoulders would shake up and down.

We also used to try to get him to point to pictures in books. We would tell him what it was and try to get him to repeat what we were saying. He never did respond positively despite our untiring efforts over many years. He loved us doing things like that with him. So did we.

Mum would sometimes be at the kitchen window and see Rock walking down the street outside our house pushing my dolls pram. He would often get out and push my dolls pram down Nursery Ridge Road in Redcliffs when we moved there.

He became annoyed when he saw Margaret knitting. If she happened to be sitting near him whilst knitting, he would patiently wait his opportunity, as always, then quickly pull the stitches off the needle and laugh. He thought he was quite funny on these occasions.

I remember him walking around the back yard a lot on his own. He always had something in his hand, continuously tapping his tongue; he actually wore out many sticks, even wooden coat hangers with this practice.

Rock used to hug us all very tight, say 'aah' and laugh. He would not let go until he was ready. We used to love him doing that.

Most Down's syndrome people are quite affectionate. Rock was, and he knew how to be gentle with babies and small children.

He always loved the company of children; he would laugh with them while they were playing in the room with him.

Margaret and her husband Lothar's eldest son Robert used to love sitting on the front step of the house beside Rock while Rock would gently pat him on the head.

When my own children were still babies, I often sat them on his knee. When he was satisfied, the nurse had taken place long enough he would gently lift his arms up to let me know he had finished his hold.

Once while living at Wentworth in New South Wales mum came in from being outside one day and found the kitchen tap was running freely into the sink. She was puzzled as to how this happened as she turned it off. Water is a scarce commodity in Wentworth and everybody living there are quite aware as to the need for conservation. On another occasion, it happened again but this time she also noticed an empty glass on the sink and the kitchen cabinet sliding glass door was open. It did not take long for her to work out that it must have been Rock getting up off his chair and getting himself a drink, as he was the only other person in the house at the time.

He continued doing this for some time but one day he just stopped doing it and was never to repeat it ever again for the remainder of his life.

Mum and I used to take Rock for a walk down to the Darling River that ran along the backyard of our house at Wentworth. He always needed a rest before attempting the walk back as we had to climb the levy bank constructed along the river to protect residents from high water when it occasionally flooded.

Dad moved to Tasmania to live with Brian in his final years. When close to death all our family living on the mainland went to Tasmania to visit him before he died. During the boat trip over the engines suddenly stopped and all the lights went out. We were all in our cabin at the time and became that frightened we all ran up on deck to see what the problem was. The only lighting was in the stairways and that was quite dim. When we arrived up top we sat down on the deck before realising, we had left poor Rockney behind in the cabin alone!

My husband Peter was sleeping on the couch one day when we had Rock staying at our house. He obviously didn't want Peter to fall asleep as he kept going over to him and almost sitting on his face. I kept bringing him back to his chair but every time I left the room, I'd find Rock creeping back along the floor on his bottom heading straight to the sleeping Peter. He would look up at Peter for a while then raise himself up to sit up close to Peter's head, right on the tip of the couch as if to say, 'Well are you going to move or not?'

Whenever Barbara and her husband Bob would come to take Rock back after him spending some time with my family, Bob would come in the front door and while walking toward Rock would gruffly say to him, 'Come on Smithy, get off your backside you little bludger and get in the car'. Rock would laugh like mad. He seemed to appreciate the way Bob spoke to him.

They sincerely enjoyed each other's company.[1]

---

1 Lynette Black to Brian Smith, email, April 2009, original in authors in possession.

The Decision

ON one occasion while Barbara was away, Lynette was looking after Rocky at her home in Chaffey Avenue in Merbein, a nearby township to the City of Mildura. The Christie Centre bus was supposed to drop Rock off at her house no later than 4.30 in the afternoon. Four-thirty came and went and Lynette became concerned, as he had not been dropped off as planned. She rang the Christie Centre to make enquiries as to his whereabouts. All they could do was to confirm the understanding that he was indeed due to be dropped off as planned at around 4.30 pm, but as the bus had not returned to the centre after taking all the clients home from their day's activities at that stage, the person on the other end of the phone could not help her any further. A while later the bus did turn up with Rocky the only client passenger left on board. The chaperone woman on the bus explained that they had mistaken the address and had taken him to Chaffey Avenue in Mildura. When they had tried to get Rock off the bus at that address, he steadfastly refused to leave his seat. She ultimately went into the house they had stopped at only to find out themselves it was the wrong address. She then realised the right address must have been in the adjoining town of Merbein, which also had a Chaffey Street.

Immediately Lynette entered the bus, Rock took her hand and left without any fuss whatsoever. The woman commented that Rocky obviously knew he was at the wrong address previously.

On another occasion, a carer at the Christie Centre was teaching Rock how to splash his hands in a bowl of water. When finished with her instructions she turned to walk away only to experience an object suddenly hitting her on the backside followed by the onset of dampness. Rock had hurled the bowl of water at her as she left. His reaction was the usual bout of uncontrolled laughter.

As he aged, he became more susceptible to illness. He fell off a chair at the Christie Centre and broke a leg but recovered quickly.

Things became more serious when he was apparently in great pain over many weeks. He would continually moan and his eyes showed fear. Doctors couldn't ascertain what the cause was nor could his specialists and of course, Rocky couldn't explain anything to them either. As his condition worsened, Barbara insisted that, an x-ray of his abdomen be undertaken. As a result, a large abnormal shadow appeared resulting in a diagnosis that his bladder was frightfully extended and was pushing one of his kidneys to one side.

An operation to correct the anomaly was quickly arranged, as it was determined that his bladder had not been emptying properly. The excess fluid was removed and from then on, he had to deal with a catheter.

Rock was now nearing his sixth decade, a long innings for a person with Down's Syndrome, when he suddenly and frighteningly developed epilepsy.

His fits became quite regular and his sister Barbara became most concerned.

In his latter years pneumonia set in regularly also and as a result, he was often hospitalised. Each time he became weaker and on many occasions it appeared that he would die. His extraordinary will to live however brought him back from the brink even after he had to get his fluids through a drip.

At this stage, he became that weak that he had to be supported by pillows to prevent him rolling over. He could walk no more, nor could he sit up without being assisted. He showed little interest in what was going on around him although he showed signs that he still recognised Barbara and his eyes brightened when he heard children enter his room.

Nearing the finish he was unable and unwilling to eat any solids and it was proposed to have him force-fed food through another tube to keep him alive.

Barbara contacted his siblings seeking their thoughts on what steps should be taken concerning his future as his doctor and the specialist treating him were giving conflicting advise on his prognosis following the insertion of a 'peg' that would be required for force feeding purposes. This procedure is carried out surgically while the patient is under general anaesthesia (asleep and pain-free). A small, flexible, hollow tube with a balloon or special tip is inserted into the stomach through a small cut on the left side of the belly area. The surgeon uses stitches to close the stomach around the tube as well as the cut.

One doctor would advise that the procedure should be carried out to prolong his life while the other advised against it stating that such a move would be inhumane and only serve to prolong an already deteriorating quality of life.

It was felt that he should not have to suffer anymore. We agreed not to subject him to having a 'peg' installed for the purposes of having food forced upon him against his will. A decision, we were all fully aware of, that would soon bring about the end of his life.

It was not an easy decision to come to but it was a necessary one. We considered carefully all aspects of what some would call euthanasia and were careful to involve operatives from Palliative Care fully in our decision. Palliative Care personnel were considerate and encouraging in their support and advised as to what to expect from Rocky over the coming days and possibly a week or so. His body organs were to slowly break down and cease operating until no life was to be left in his body for it to exist further. All the family came together to be with Rocky for his last days with us. None of us were prepared for what was to finally eventuate!

The Transformation

I WAS at home in Devonport, Tasmania, when I received a phone call from my sister Barbara

"Brian," she said softly "I think the end is near for Rocky."

"What has happened Barbara," I replied apprehensively. Although, I was aware that Rocky had been seriously ill. I had received a similar phone call at about the same time for the previous two years running. I had dropped everything and went across to the mainland to be with him and the rest of the family, fearing the worst each time. Each time I would return with Rocky miraculously recovering at the last minute. Each time he became weaker and it was hard to believe that he could become any weaker and still live.

"He is now refusing food and fluids, Brian," she said, as I was evaluating the sombre tone of her voice. She went on to say that the doctor wanted to introduce force feeding by inserting what they call a 'peg' directly into his stomach.

"This would ensure that he received enough nutrition to stay alive," she said. I could clearly pick up the emotion in her voice.

"One of the specialists told me that it would be inhumane to force him to live any longer," she revealed in a sobbing like tone.

Then came the explosive question,

"What do you think we should do Brian?" I suddenly realised the completely unfair position she had been placed in. It is easy to have an opinion when you have no responsibility as to the consequences, but when it is brought home to you that whatever you might say in a situation like this a persons life may well depend on it, and on this occasion it was to be that of our own brother.

Rocky had been refusing fluids well before this and had been placed on a drip to ensure he remained hydrated but the difficulty Barbara was now experiencing in feeding him was a most serious development. He had been getting lighter and lighter over the last couple of years until now there was almost nothing of him left.

I thought long and hard and then I said,

"I think it would be cruel to force food into him Barbara when he obviously doesn't want it."

The words rang in my ears as I spoke them. I couldn't believe what I had just said and it actually hurt, I felt pressure on my temples and my head throbbed. I then heard Barbara answer.

"Yes Brian, I agree, it would be cruel to keep him alive any longer." I then told her that I would come over there to be with them both.

When I arrived in Mildura I was picked up at the airport and taken straight to the hospital where Rocky had been admitted so that doctors could regain control of his seizures as Barbara couldn't get any medication into him, to ensure his epilepsy was under control, because of his adamant refusal to allow anything past his lips.

On arrival at the hospital it was sad to see the state he was in. he was lying on his back quite motionless, with his eyes shut and breathing very deeply. His cheeks were drawn in and he was quite pale. I don't think he recognised that I was there but the rest of his family were all with him wishing him well. All were aware that the decision had been made to not have the 'peg' inserted to force food into him against his will. All knew that he was condemned to die within the next few days, a week at the most. And all appeared content with the decision that had been made.

The next day after his epilepsy had been brought under control Barbara told the hospital authorities that she was taking him home to allow him to spend his last days in familiar surroundings. She and I then went to seek out the most comfortable bed possible for him to lie in during those final days. We wanted him to be as comfortable as possible. The bed we acquired was the latest in technological development. It softly vibrated, it folded, it lowered and raised, all with the press of a button.

We had no sooner got the bed organised when we heard that the ambulance was on its way to bring him home. Once settled in his new bed he looked comfortable and relaxed and we all felt certain that he knew he was home again. All his siblings were with him and we all determined to remain with him till the last.

Change was slow but his breathing became more laboured as time passed and he showed no interest in wanting any food or water although we kept his mouth moist at all times with a damp cloth. The doctor would call in regularly and administer injections that kept him calm and his epilepsy under control. Palliative care nurses also called in each day to oversee his condition but his awareness of what was going on around him was not obvious to detect.

There were few occasions when he was alone, usually two or three of us were with him at any one time and even during the night hours someone volunteered to stay with him in case he became distressed or was to pass away alone.

Early on one of these mornings we had all congregated in Rocky's room with him before dispersing for breakfast. Lynette, who had spent the entire night in the room, asked Barbara if she could borrow her car to go home for a shower and a change of clothes. Barbara agreed and went to another part of the house and returned to hand her the keys of the car. Lynette took the keys and was the first to leave the room. Barbara then followed to attend to some washing up chores at the kitchen sink. Margaret and I then left the room together to sit in the adjoining dining room to talk. This left Rocky alone in his room for what was possibly the first time since he returned from the hospital. All was quiet and Rocky's laboured breathing could be clearly heard in the background, when he suddenly emitted a different sound. It could have been a cough or a grunt but it was out of the ordinary enough for all of us to hear and to attend him immediately. Lynette who was outside the house but had not left the premises at that stage noticed the activity taking place and returned inside.

When we assembled around his bed all appeared normal. He was lying on his back with his eyes closed. The bedclothes were pulled up to about his mid chest and he was motionless. His breathing was not prominent enough to be noticeable but he was definitely breathing. Slowly, before our eyes, we noticed his appearance changing. It was that slow you could not see it happening but his features were indeed dissolving into someone different. His tongue that had hitherto been a main feature of his appearance because of it being quite large. Too large to fit inside his mouth. And because of it being exposed to the open air for 60 years it had also become toughened and quite rough. It was now gone! It could not have been inside his mouth because his cheeks were not extended. Quite the opposite, in that the skin of his face itself was now smooth and tight, his large lips were becoming smaller and clearly defined. His eyebrows were no longer bushy but pencil fine, the pronounced bony ridge above his eyes disappeared and he had a small smooth and rounded forehead. His hair was fine and darker and it even gave the appearance of having been brushed. His neck became small in proportion to his other features and the loose skin around his throat was gone. He appeared quite young, extremely good looking and perfectly proportioned. Even his shoulders were in conformity to his small youthful face. I mentioned to the others that I felt he looked like a real little dandy.

"Put a top hat on him and you could take him to the races," I think I said.

He remained like this for some time while we freely chatted and commented on what he looked like. The strangest thing of all was that we were all accepting the changes as being normal. None of us became excited as we nonchalantly took it all in and accepted it for what it was, a miracle! But we were fully accepting it as being quite possible and a normal occurrence. None of us questioned what was happening.

After a time his new appearance slowly dissolved away and he once again became the Rocky we all grew up with and knew. His tongue re-appeared first. It couldn't be seen emerging from his closed mouth, It simply very slowly started to appear. All his other features slowly followed although you couldn't see the changes occurring. It was like steam dissolving into the air. You can't see it happening but it happens none-the-less.

The transformation only occurred the once and two days later he died.

My sister Lynette who was present at the time takes up the story here in her own words.

ON Sunday April 10, 2005, Rock had an epileptic fit at about 4pm. About an hour later, he had another. Barbara rang Margaret and Margaret rang me saying she thought this may mean the end is near for Rockney.
"I'm coming in," she said.
I dropped everything and went directly to Barbara and Bob's house.

The ambulance arrived soon after to take Rock to hospital to see if there was anything, they could do there to prevent him having more fits. It was obvious he was not strong enough to handle them anymore. He had not eaten a proper meal for the last six weeks and before that, he had not eaten very much either. He had been holding his mouth tightly shut when anybody tried to feed him. He had started doing the same for drinks. Even refusing his medication.

When he started refusing drinks, Barbara rang his doctor, Dr Buckley, for advice.

The doctor introduced fluids into him via a 'drip'. The same doctor had put him on a 'drip' about 18 months previously, when he developed pneumonia and was at such a very low ebb that none of us thought he could recover. He did recover however but it took a lot out of him.

A few days before Rocky's latest hospitalisation he suffered a coughing fit, Barbara rang palliative care at the Mildura hospital, she said they advised her it was possible too much fluid may have built up in his lungs, so she took the fluids off him to see if there was any improvement.

With Rock back in hospital again us three sisters spent the next few nights and days at the hospital with him. Brian flew over from Tasmania.

A few days later Rock returned home from the hospital as Barbara wished him to spend his last days with us at home where she knew he was more content, rather than pass away in the more clinical atmosphere of the hospital.

For the rest of his life with us, Margaret, Brian, and I moved into Barbara and Bob's house with Rocky.

During this last week, Rockney had all five siblings together for the first time in many years.

Two days before Rockney was to pass away, I had decided to go home to my place, which was not far away, for a shower. It was 6.25am. I went outside to drive Barbara's car to my home, as she had allowed me to borrow it, but I could not get it into reverse gear, to allow me to back the car out of the carport and onto the road.

As I looked up towards Rock's bedroom window that was alongside the carport, I saw Margaret, Brian and Barbara walk past, all hurriedly going into Rock's room. I immediately thought the worse and alighted from the car to re enter the house.

When I got into Rock's room, I asked what had happened.

"I was sitting at the dining room table with Margaret," Brian said, "Barbara was at the kitchen sink. We all heard him make a coughing sound so we all came in together to investigate," he added.

The four of us were standing by his bed watching him struggle to breathe. Each time he drew breath it made a deep indentation in his neck just above his collarbone.

What occurred next astounded all of us!

I said to the others standing there with me, "His face is changing!"

Brian answered, "Can you see that too, I thought I was imagining it!

We all stood there watching over him in utmost amazement noting all the changes taking place in his appearance before our eyes.

He looked like someone we had never seen before. As his features changed, we spoke about it amongst each other. It began when his mouth closed. He had lived with his tongue hanging out from his mouth pretty well all his life. It had become quite rough over the years and it was too large for the confines of his mouth, but it was miraculously gone now, it was all inside his mouth and his cheeks were not puffed out by it being there. He had assumed perfectly shaped lips. A beautiful little, if slightly pointed nose. His eyes were shut but his eye sockets, eyebrows; cheeks and forehead were absolutely perfectly proportioned. The deep ridge above his eyebrows was gone.

His forehead looked as smooth as silk, no wrinkles whatsoever. His throat had no skin hanging from it. His shoulders fitted in perfectly in proportion to his beautiful little face. He looked like a boy of about five or six years of age.

The Down's syndrome look was completely gone.

Brian commented how beautiful he looked saying, "If you put a bow tie and hat on him he could go to the races, he looks a real little dandy!"

It was completely inexplicable but beautiful to witness.

After a while, his face slowly changed back to what he normally *looked like. His tongue came out of his mouth, his lips thickened, his forehead wrinkled and loose skin once again dropped from his chin. His Down's syndrome appearance returned as did his laboured breathing.*

None of us is sure how long this transformation took but it appeared to be quite a period. His changed appearance remained for some little time probably 10 or 15 minutes. While it was so, we were free to touch him and freely comment amongst ourselves about the changes taking place.[2]

My sister Barbara was caring for Rock, up to, and when, he passed away. These are her words explaining that remarkable period:

Rock was eating next to nothing by now. A few weeks into March, he stopped eating altogether, and would only let me give him small sips of drink. I was so worried that I asked the palliative care nurse if he could go on the drip. Although it is only saline, I thought it might help him feel better. She rang Dr. Buckley and he agreed.

For a few weeks, I would connect it up in the morning and disconnect it when it finished. At least it was something. Within a short while, he refused to eat or drink anything at all

I was so worried about him not getting his epilepsy medication but was advised there was nothing they could do. He was becoming so thin I was noticing a big difference every day and I could do nothing about it.

I would look at him propped up with cushions and felt so frustrated. It hurt so much.

Palliative Care was supportive.

One day I was working on the computer where Rock could see me. I suddenly heard a giggle. I looked towards him. He was looking directly at me and laughing. I was so surprised I said. "Are you

2 Lynette Black to Brian Smith, email, April 2009, original in authors in possession.

laughing at me?" I went over to him and he had the biggest smile on his face and such a happy look in his eyes. I hugged him and played with him telling him he was a 'good boy', until he once again dozed off.

Sadly that was the last time he laughed. It proved to me how happy he was to be where he was and to have me with him. It made me feel good.

One Saturday afternoon after he had been on the drip for a couple of weeks he began to cough and the gurgle in his chest was terrible to hear. He was quite distressed so I rang palliative care and the lady on duty told me to take the drip off him. She told me I was going against nature and his body was breaking down and was unable to cope with the fluid. I didn't want to hear it but I knew she was right. I had all sorts of thoughts running through my head.

The next day he became very agitated in the early afternoon. I couldn't calm him. He suddenly went into an epileptic seizure. An hour later, he had another one and he wasn't coming out of it properly. Palliative care came around and I agreed he would have to go to hospital to have the seizures stopped. Of course, I went with him and Margaret and Lynny came up later.

He had to be admitted into the hospital until they could get his medication right to stop the fits. They told us he would have to stay for two nights and each night they told us he might not make it through to morning. Of course, Margaret, Lynny, and I slept in the room with him. They attached a pump to him to administer morphine and another medication to calm him, as he needed it. Brian came over on the Monday night.

I finally told the hospital doctors that I was taking him home and that was that. I knew without a doubt that he would want to be home where he was loved. He proved to us so many times that it was a place where he was happy. They agreed and sent him home in an ambulance.

Once Rock was home, palliative care nurses came in to see him every day.

Margaret, Brian, Lynny, Bob, and I were all with Rock day and night. My daughter Sharon cooked for us each night.

Rock grew weaker each day. My grandchildren, Nikkita, Brock,

Mikkaela, Tahlia, Rebekah and Sarah wrote down their thoughts of Rock. I was so touched at the beautiful things they said. I put them on the wall beside Rocks bed. It really bought home how much they loved him. Rock was so sick and they came in every now and then, kissed him, and held his hand. They cried every now and then. They had a complete understanding of what was happening. I'm sure Rock knew they were there.

I kept telling him he was home. I hope he understood because it would have meant a lot to him.

On about the third day home from the hospital, early in the morning, one of the few times no one was in the room with Rock, we heard him cough. We rushed into his room and couldn't believe what we saw. Before our eyes, Rock was changing.

His whole appearance was changing.

His Downs syndrome features were slowly changing, his skin became smooth, his eyebrows became defined, and his lips were small and perfect. His nose was perfect. He appeared much younger. Even his shoulders were in proportion with his perfect little face. Margaret, Brian, Lynny, and I looked at him from all angles for about twenty minutes. We couldn't believe the transformation that took place.

As we were looking at him, his appearance gradually returned to the Rocky we knew.

What actually happened we don't know. Later however we looked at some younger photos of him and could see a likeness.

I think it was the next day Rock went into a deep coma and palliative care nurses told us his internal organs had broken down but he kept breathing.

Dr Buckley came in each night and thought he would get a call during that night but Rock would not give in.

I kept whispering to him that it was OK to go, to go to be with mum, that I would be alright. I told him repeatedly, and then early on the Sunday morning I thought, "Maybe he doesn't understand what I am saying." Therefore, I asked God to help him understand.

He took his last breath an hour and a half later.

We were all there with him and I had my arms around him. I told him it was OK and felt great relief for him.

His last peaceful breath occurred on the morning of Sunday the 17th
of April 2005.
He was 61 years of age.[3]

***

Dr Buckley attended to certify his death. After examining Rockney's lifeless body, he left the room and came over to me where I was standing in the dining room.

"There is a bit of a problem Brian," he said.

"In what way?" I replied rather surprised.

"Rockney has died of malnutrition and no one should die of malnutrition in this day and age in Australia. I don't know what to put on the death certificate."

---

3 Barbara Andrews to Brian Smith, email,2009, original in author's possession.

Search for the Truth

IN our effort to understand what had occurred to Rockney on the morning of his transformation, two of my sisters, Margaret and Lynette, and I, organised an interview with Father Monahan in Mildura.

We chose Father Monahan because he was the oldest priest in the district, being over 80 years of age, and we thought that his years of service in the church might well have had him hear of something similar happening to someone else at some other time in his long serving past. We also chose the Catholic Church to talk to, as we believed that members of the Catholic Church believed that a person's physical features could change horrifically when possessed by evil spirits. We reasoned if that was true then a priest of the church might well believe that a persons features may also be capable of change for the better if possessed by good spirits.

He told us that he had never heard of such a phenomena in his entire career in the priesthood, nor had he ever read of such an occurrence happening.

We were disappointed with what we heard but were pleased to accept his honesty.

I then contacted internationally known spiritualist Patrick Rodriguez for his views.

"Unfortunately, I cannot say with any certainty what it is that you experienced. I believe that I have experienced similar things but this seems to be unique," he said.

"When I have done Past Life Regression using hypnosis this does happen, where I can see a face that is almost superimposed on the face of the person. If I try to analyse what's happening it then disappears but when I just allow it I can see it clearly," he added.

"I also see this when working with mediums who are doing channelling. As the medium takes on the personality of a spirit, her face may become superimposed with the face of another person."

"Again, I can't really say what happened to your brother. These have only been my experiences," he concluded.

Although not helping that much in Rocky's case, his mention of the occasions when another face appears to impose itself on that of another did interest me. I felt it was an area worth investigating further.

There are now many recorded cases where, under hypnosis, a subject has not only recounted details from what appears to be a previous life, but also spoken a foreign language of which they claimed to have little or no previous knowledge.

A notable case of this is the famous Hollywood actor Glenn Ford. Under hypnosis, he recalled five previous lives – one in particular as a French cavalryman under Louis XIV. The astonishing part was that though Ford said he knew only a few basic phrases in French, under hypnosis he spoke French with ease while describing this life. In addition, when recordings of his regression were sent to UCLA (University of California), they discovered that not only was Ford speaking fluent French, he was in fact speaking the Parisian dialect from the 17th century.
Jane Evans, a Welsh housewife, agreed to be filmed for BBC television being regressed back to a past life by Arnell Bloxham, president of the British Society of Hypnotherapists and a respected practitioner. She had originally consulted him about rheumatism and under hypnosis, revealed seven past lives including one life - where the regression was televised - where she identified herself as a Jewish

woman living in the city of York in 12th century England. She described many details of Jewish life at the time and how she and the local Jews were forced to wear badges to identify themselves. She also spoke of a terrible massacre of the Jewish population by the local townspeople. During this event, she recalled taking shelter with her children in the crypt of a local church, but they were discovered by the mob and that is where she died. Professor Barrie Dobson, an expert on Jewish history at York University, was called in to check the information from her memories. He found that her description of 12th century Jewish life was impressive with its accuracy and in fact, he was convinced that some of the details would have only been known to professional historians. However, it also seemed that some details appeared to be quite incorrect. Firstly, it was not until the 13th century (1215 to be precise) that the Church authorities in Rome decreed that Jews in Christian countries were to wear special identification. Secondly, from her description, the church had to have been St. Mary's Castlegate, but it did not have a crypt. However further investigation revealed that the practice of making Jews wear identification was already widespread in England during the 12th century before the church decree. Then astonishingly several months later, during renovation of the church a sealed chamber was discovered below the floor, which appeared to have been a crypt – a very rare phenomenon indeed for churches in the area. So not only did her regression bring forth obscure details which were historically accurate, it also yielded historical information which should most definitely not have been available at that time.

Often the first hint about a past life people have is an inexplicable interest in a particular country, language, time-period, historical event, etc. In addition, often when presented with photographs or movie footage, which related to their past life, they might feel an emotional rush and even identify themselves somehow with what they are seeing.

For example, an English TV documentary showed an American who had become so fascinated with the American Civil War that he had turned his house into a Civil War museum. Not surprisingly, under hypnosis he remembered being a soldier in the Civil War. This can be *viewed by the sceptic as wishful thinking, but conversely it follows that a Civil War veteran would always have a fascination for that period – probably even into their next incarnation.*

Recurring dreams or nightmares are a common way people claim to be able to view their past lives. This can vary between vague dreams of an unpleasant nature with a recurring theme all the way through to vivid dreams where other participants can be clearly recognised.

Some people have seemingly irrational fears from a young age for such things as drowning, aircraft crashing, loud noises, etc. Often when trying to work through this problem under hypnosis, the person will state that the cause of their phobia is an event from a time when they were someone else – and often the event is the cause of their death in that life.

Another problem that can occur is when people have a chronic health problem for which there seems to be no evident reason. Here again, when working through this problem under hypnosis, sometimes people will state that the origin of their problem is a traumatic event from a past life. And surprisingly once this discovery is made (under trance, etc), the person's problems are often reported as – almost miraculously - going away of their own accord

The area of children's past lives is quite remarkable – especially in western countries, where children have seldom been exposed to the concept of reincarnation. Often such memories can fade as some grow up, while others will be able to recall past incarnations all their life. Thousands of cases have been documented by various researchers from around the world and some children are recorded as having described their past life residence and recognised family members by name – even when these families live in a different district – and even successfully passed tests set by the identified family. What is remarkable here is that in most cases the children appear to have no incentive, financial or otherwise, to make such claims. Dr Ian Stevenson, Director of Personality Studies at the University of Virginia, has devoted the last forty years to the scientific documentation of past life memories (without hypnosis) of children from all over the world – and has over 3,000 cases in his files.[4]

However interesting these reported cases may be, none of them mentioned an occasion where the physical features of a person actually changed, therefore defying all logic and the law of physics itself. Rockney could never be hypnotised, but his incarnation into his unfortunate life was surely not common and I felt my thoughts leading me to question the realm of possession.

.

---

4 Olive Ray and Robin Evans of The Lowestoft Spiritual Centre, Gt. Yarmouth, G.B.
http://www.lowestoftspiritualcentre.co.uk, accessed 2009.

The Supposition

"If we limit ourselves to thinking in terms of realities, facts, and knowledge, we have got the future all wrong because it is made, not of certainties, but of dreams. The future does not exist in the physical world but is present in our thoughts and dreams only...Far too many companies search for the future in the rear-view mirror, because that is where certainties are found. There we find the part of reality that can be verified. The strict scientific model of logic is a trap that prevents us from looking ahead." - Rolf Jensen.

THE more I found myself searching for an explanation on what happened to Rockney before he died the more I began to understand that I was doomed to failure. It was then that I came across the above quote from Rolf Jensen.

I too, like everybody else I had enquired enlightenment from, was guilty of thinking in terms of reality. In reality, Rocky's change of physical appearance was not possible, honourable devout religious people, spiritualists and others laying claim to having an understanding of such things were left without an explanation. It then dawned on me that we are all limited in our understanding because knowledge is heavily weighted by us having to have the data of some kind of factual happenings of past events to rely on. I myself was guilty of looking for someone having a factual knowledge of knowing, seeing or hearing of something similar happening to somebody else in the past to prove my own sanity to myself. What we see has to be verified before it becomes believable and how could the unverifiable be seen as being real?

I felt that Jensen was onto something. If I had witnessed Rockneys transformation alone, I possibly would have kept the matter to myself, thinking I must have been hallucinating. The fact that my three sisters were there with me at the time and we openly discussed his changing features among ourselves whilst it was actually taking place made a lot of difference. We could not have all been hallucinating at the same time. Lynette, who was on her way home would not have been there if the car had have started and of course, she did not return simply to hallucinate with us. What we witnessed was indeed real. Not physically possible, but real, never the less.

'The strict scientific model of logic is a trap that prevents us from looking ahead,' Jensen had said. I had been guilty of exactly that. I would never find out what happened that day if I kept looking back searching for an explanation.

If Rockneys change of appearance occurred because he wanted to show us how he would appear in the 'after-life,' as some suggested, it would indeed be sad. That would mean he had to live his 61 years as an invalid but in his last two days he was allowed to appear 'normal' to his siblings, siblings who loved him anyway, no matter how he physically appeared to them. It would be doubly cruel as this change of appearance only lasted 20 minutes at the most and he then changed back to his normal appearance once again.

In my search for the truth, I came across many people who have made the supernatural their life study. Many claim to be able to converse with the spirit world and I have covered some such instances in this writing. There are many recorded instances of interaction between earth bound spirits and living persons and I finally developed the thought that we exist much closer to each other's realm of existence than many of us believe. I decided to throw logic out the window and finally accept the fact that not all happenings in this physical world of ours can be explained logically.

I had earlier contacted well-known spiritualist Patrick Rodriguez and he said he could not help me. However, I did remember a quote from him that led me into a train of thought that I found was developing strongly within me, regarding the different kinds of spiritual possessions that are believed to take place between earthbound spirits and vulnerable people from time to time.

He had said, quote:

> "An attached spirit is when an earthbound spirit is attracted to a living person and then begins to "hang out" with the living person. After a while, the spirit finds that they become emotionally attached. Often the spirit will feel safe or even complacent about being with the person.
> In most cases, attached spirits don't have any ill-will and they don't mean to harm the person. It's almost always just that the spirit had some connection to the person, either emotionally, similar life-experiences, or the spirit could have known the person in life or even a past life." Unquote.

My sisters and I had concluded that Rockney's changed features resembled a photograph we had of him when he was about nine years old. It was a photograph that showed no signs whatsoever of him having Downs Syndrome. His features were small and sharp. It was the only photograph we had of him that went close to what we saw on that memorable morning. I found myself having to work out why it was this particular likeness we saw that day. What was so important at that stage in his life that this likeness returned to him only two days before his physical body was to die?

Our elder brother Max, whom our parents had adopted as a baby, died in 1945 at the age of 16 years. He contracted Meningitis at the age of two leaving him backward mentally and prone to epileptic fits. He never attended school.

He was aware of his disabilities and was hurt when shunned by his peers. When our mother bore the twins, Barbara and Rockney, in 1943, Max was 14 and he adored the newcomers to the family. In fact the last words he spoke before he died were.

"When I get better, can I play with the twins again?"

I have been told by spiritualists, during the course of research for this book, that when we die it is usual for a spirit from the 'other side', a family friend or a loved one who has earlier passed on, to meet with the new spirit crossing over to assist in whatever changes are required. We are also told that on the rare occasion, the spirit crossing over is sometimes confused and either doesn't want to finish the process of 'crossing over' or doesn't know how. It is on these occasions that the 'new' spirit becomes, what is called, 'an earth bound spirit.'

Max was an ideal prospect to fall into the latter category. He had no family members available to 'welcome' him to the other side, other than a cousin who had passed away not all that long beforehand, but she was an infant herself and may have been unable to assist. Our parents had moved from their home state of Tasmania to Victoria where Max passed away. He was also very closely attached to the family emotionally, especially the new twins, and even more so to Rockney who was, like himself, considerably disabled.

It is not hard to imagine Max, under these unique circumstances, clinging to the family he loved and not wanting to 'go it alone' into the wider spirit world.

I feel it appropriate here that I repeat the statement given to me by the psychic whom I quoted previously:

> "An attached spirit is when an earthbound spirit is attracted to a living person and then begins to "hang out" with the living person. After a while, the spirit finds that they become emotionally attached. Often the spirit will feel safe or even complacent about being with the person.
> In most cases, attached spirits don't have any ill-will and they don't mean to harm the person. It's almost always just that the spirit had some connection to the person, either emotionally, similar life-experiences, or the spirit could have known the person in life or even a past life."

Could it be envisaged that Max became an earth bound spirit and attached himself to Rockney as he found comfort in such an association.

This close 'hanging out' association continued for seven years when something occurred to allow Max to share Rockney's physical body with him absolutely, from that day on, until Rockney's death some 50 years later. It was around this time that Rocky started walking, about nine years old, and because of his physical condition he looked no more than four or five years old. The same age when the photograph of him was taken that recorded an appearance similar to the transformation of appearance we witnessed before his death.

Could it be that Rockney himself didn't age from that time onward? His body did, as we all witnessed over the ensuring years but could it be that his spirit didn't.

In Rockney's later years he became quite ill as has been recorded earlier in this writing but something always brought him back from the brink of dying at the eleventh hour, when all hope of saving him had been given up.

On this last occasion when his body did actually die, it was different.

Doctors had suggested force-feeding him to prolong his life but we siblings agreed among ourselves that it would be too cruel to allow his continued suffering and it would be best to not force food or fluids upon him anymore against his will.

In effect, we allowed his body to close down through a lack of sufficient nutrition. There was to be no reprieve at the last minute on this occasion.

Nearing the end of his second week without nourishment of any manner, his features changed temporarily in our presence and we saw Rockney of about nine years of age but with skin that took on the hue and appearance of ivory, take over the physical appearance of his 61 tear old invalid body lying in his sick bed.

Could it be that we four siblings were witnessing Rockney leaving the body he had been trapped in for all those years? Did he leave as a nine-year-old boy?

Two days later, his 61 year old body was to quietly pass away and could it be that was when Max's spirit also, after all those years, had finally found its way to the other side, no doubt assisted by Rockney himself and our parents whose spirits were finally all together again, their earthly journey complete.

This synopsis may well have merit but it still leaves too many unknowns. There is no way of testing its accuracy therefore it must forever rest in the realm of assumption.

"It may be that child prodigies are a result of such spirit influence."
I read this statement in a report on spiritual effects on certain people I was researching and it struck a chord immediately.

"Dr. Charles Richet, the 1913 Nobel Prize winner in medicine, reported on the strange case of Pepito Arriola, when, at age 3 years, 3 months, he performed at the Psychological Congress in Paris during 1900.

Richet stated that the boy played brilliantly on the piano. "He composed military or funeral marches, waltzes, habaneras, minuets, and played some twenty difficult pieces from memory," Richet, a professor of physiology at the medical school of the University of Paris for 38 years, wrote. "A hundred members of the Congress heard and applauded him."

It was further reported that little Pepito's hands could not stretch more than five notes, yet he appeared to sound full octaves. Some onlookers said that his hands seemed to increase in size during the playing, and Rosalie Thompson, a clairvoyant, claimed that she saw the child dissolve into the figure of a man while at the piano."

I instantly sent a copy of this report to my sisters to gauge their feelings.

We were all immediately struck by the usage of the word 'dissolve' that was used by the clairvoyant Rosalie Thompson in her description of the phenomena she had witnessed.

Only people who had actually witnessed a similar happening would have 'picked up' on the significance of using that one little word.

In our descriptions on what happened to our brother's body, none of us thought to use the word 'dissolve' to describe the event, yet it was the perfect word to explain what occurred on that day.

There is no doubt, Rockneys features slowly dissolved into that of a young child and after a short period of stability the boy's features slowly dissolved back into the appearance of the 61 year old invalid man that he was.

Rosalie must have seen a transformation take place as we did.

We wondered why others witnessing the child's performance did not see what was occurring before their very eyes, when in our case we all saw exactly the same thing at the same time while we were immediately adjacent to Rockney's body.

Some people at the performance claimed they saw the hands of the child pianist enlarge themselves. Perhaps more saw exactly what happened but their minds refused to accept the impossible and therefore blocked it out.

I remember the day my son Craige died. The three injured footballers were transported to the local hospital by ambulance. Being a small country hospital, there was initially insufficient space available to accommodate them all in the surgery at the same time. Craige was temporarily placed on a stretcher in the foyer of the hospital while room for him inside was urgently being organised. I was seated in the same foyer, only a yard or so from him, but I failed to recognise him. When speaking about the situation later I remember saying that I thought the body on the stretcher was bandaged up to such a degree that I didn't know who it was. In fact, his unconscious body actually appeared uninjured on the outside. He had no bandages on him. He died from a torn aorta that ensured a massive loss of blood was escaping into his chest cavity. Apparently, my mind was refusing to believe the situation that I was otherwise being forced to come to terms with on that day.

Is life itself but a mirage? Is it that we predominately see what we want to see? But, in fact there is constantly much more going on around us than we realise that remains unseen.

My mother swore all her life that she saw Max's spirit leave the day he died at our home at Bonbeach near Melbourne. I definitely saw a man standing in the centre of the road before I collided with him in the army bus I was driving that tragic night near Mornington in country Victoria. My three sisters and I watched as Rocky's appearance dissolved from an elderly invalid to a bright faced child then slowly dissolve back into his usual self once again.

After all Rolf Jensen had previously stated:

"The strict scientific model of logic is a trap that prevents us from looking ahead." [5] [6]

---

5 Rolf Jensen, *The Dream Society: How the Coming*, http://groups.gaia.com_books/ accessed 2009.
6 Patrick and Melanie Rodriguez, The Soul Rescue Site, http://www.soulrescuesite.com accessed 2009.

Afterword

MANKIND has been conditioned to not be able to see into the future. Yes, Jensen was right in a previous chapter to say that the future exists only in dreams.

None of us can plan for what we will need once we have left this realm of existence. That is if we will need anything at all. Because of this conditioning, some ancient dreamers have sought to fill the void by claiming to have spoken in confidence with our maker. Such people have claimed to have undergone this feat on every continent on earth at one time or another and this has resulted in a myriad of varying religions coming into existence.

Mans differing religions have therefore given birth to fanatical adherence to their beliefs by some of their followers, because all mans religions promise a life after death if certain strict rules are complied with, and all followers want to ensure their earthly life continues into that promised afterlife.

This belief is however at the expense of non-believers, who unfortunately, are universally purported to be not allowed to partake of such a valued prize.

Such belief encourages a follower of one particular religion to claim ascendancy over another because he feels his God favours him and the life of the other ignorant believer of a different religion is of lesser importance. One can then believe that the slaughter of the ignorant is justifiable.

This is particularly noticeable with the practice of followers of the Jewish religion referring to themselves as 'the Chosen People' and Islamic followers generally calling non-followers of their religion 'Infidels'.

Although slaughter of other human beings is justifiable in their eyes, as long as those being slaughtered are not of the same religion, it is against their belief that they be allowed to take their own life, unless of course it is in the service of their chosen God. Suicide therefore, and euthanasia, is against the wishes of their God because it was he, who made them in the first place, and therefore it is only he, who can claim that life back again.

This is true of all of 'Man's' religions but what would the situation be if there was no religion at all? There would no doubt have been less killing in the world over the ages and less hatred between men generally. But what if life doesn't finish at death?

There does appear to be sufficient evidence to suggest that there exists something akin to life as we know it running parallel with us. We tend to weave it all into superstition, or coincidence, but we must seek to delve deeper and think with a freer, uncluttered, and unbiased mind. Not one influenced by the conditioning of time that has had us tightly tied to one religious bandwagon or another.

Where does life come from? We don't know yet, so let us at least be honest about it.

Where does life go? That is what should be important to every man, woman and child who have yet to face the answer to such a question. AND we all will sooner or later.

Whether a life finishes violently, abruptly, slowly, expected or unexpected, by ones own hand or by the hand of another, it does not matter. Once life finishes here, it appears to have not finished somewhere else.

How do we know this happens?

There is far too much evidence of inexplicable occurrences happening too regularly.

It does not appear to be governed by any of man's religions and all persons of good and bad earthly character appear to cross over equally.

Rocky's transformation showed that something more powerful than all of us does exist and that all suffering will eventually cease. But why did we have to take matters into our own hands before his personal suffering was to be no more? It could be that sometimes we are expected to take matters into our own hands here on our own earthly plane before a wrong can be righted.

The peaceful calm child in Rocky's deathbed showed that there is tranquillity in the midst of human physical chaos and fear of the unknown should not exist, as all will turn out for the better at the finish.

We, Rocky's siblings, as the ignorant earth bound humans that we are, have interpreted Rocky's transformation to appear as that of himself at a younger age. One can also accept the likeness to that of our late grandmother, Alice Betsy May Harrison (Hills). That being true then maybe the simple message was that he was being taken into good care, to suffer no more.

The motivation to write this disqisition came from these extraordinary, if not miraculous, events that took place just two days before the death of Rockney. The astonishing occurrences that took place at that time have remained inexplicable to my sisters and myself despite our seeking enlightenment from many quarters as has been diligently outlined.

I myself have not been a stranger to death as I have explained in the earlier chapters. I was also a sceptic regarding the supernatural, but life's experiences have gradually increased my interest and belief in the paranormal. Perhaps the early escape from my own death as a toddler gave me a subconscious interest in the subject but then again it could be that age itself focuses one's mind on the matter more sharply than it does in one's youth.

Whatever the reason may be, it remains a story that had to be recorded, because of the dual occurrences involving the possibility of a mystical entwining of two souls with the subsequent involvement of the supernatural, along with the delicate and highly controversial subject of euthanasia.

Rockney was born into this world with everything possible stacked against him and despite him never speaking a word in his entire life his funeral service held in Mildura, Australia, on Wednesday April 20, 2005 was packed to overflowing. Mourners who could not find a seat inside the funeral parlour hall packed shoulder to shoulder into the adjoining hallway and foyer.

My sisters and I had a special reason to mourn his passing because of the comfort he gave us when we were all children together. He taught us love, tolerance, and kindness. He gave us a sense of humour beyond the normal in that we laughed with him when he got himself into trouble in wrecking things that others had spent much time putting together, such as a set dinner placement on our dining room table or my sister Margaret's knitting. It showed us that the many things that most people look on as being important, e.g. the keeping up of appearances, are not really that important after all, as life goes on regardless.

We were happy and comfortable with Rock and he was happy and comfortable with us.

Some travelled long distances to pay their final respects with some arriving from interstate. Such was the respect shown to one of us who said nothing but lived his life the best he could under the circumstances afforded him in his drawing the shortest of short straws in the overwhelming lottery of life.

Who among us could stand up and say he should have been denied his life because of his afflictions when it was shown he meant so much to so many on his final day.

Rocky's life was longer than that normally experienced by others like him, a fact that is attributable to the loving care afforded him by our mother, and my sisters Barbara, Margaret and Lynette at different times during his life. I thank them for the care they gave him, particularly his twin sister Barbara who cared for him during his latter years when his physical condition became steadily worse. I particularly wish to thank Barbara's husband, the late Bob Andrews, for being the brother to Rockney that I never was.

I have put this book together with two aspects in mind. One outlines my experiences with the paranormal and the other, people who's deaths have remained in my memory for some particular reason, leading up to Rocky's own death. All these people died while Rocky lived on. People who, under other circumstances, could have offered society so much, people robbed of life at an absurd early age and people who took their own life, or had someone do it for them.

This book encourages the reader to ask him or herself if he or she really wants to take a strong stand against matters of the unknown as dogmatically as he or she may have prior to reading Rocky's story.

The book also contains a selection of available material sourced during research on the subject of dying. I have tried to leave all articles as original as possible because I do not wish to proclaim myself any more of an expert on either euthanasia, religion or the paranormal than the next person does. I now doubt if any other living being has more expertise on these subject either, despite many people exhibiting quite strong feelings supporting either side of the various arguments. My personal search for the truth attests to the universal lack of real knowledge of these matters that many experts would otherwise have us believe.

After all it was Albert Einstein who stated the following:

> "The human mind, no matter how highly trained, cannot grasp the universe. We are in the position of a little child, entering a huge library whose walls are covered to the ceiling with books in many different tongues. The child knows that someone must have written those books. It does not know who or how. It does not understand the languages in which they are written. The child notes a definite plan in the arrangement of the books, a mysterious order, which it does not comprehend, but only dimly suspects. That, it seems to me, is the attitude of the human mind, even the greatest and most cultured, toward God. We see a universe marvellously arranged, obeying certain laws, but we understand the laws only dimly. Our limited minds cannot grasp the mysterious force that sways the constellations. I am fascinated by Spinoza's Pantheism. I admire even more his contributions to modern thought. Spinoza is the greatest of modern philosophers, because he is the first philosopher who deals with the soul and the body as one, not as two separate things."[7]
> (Benedict Spinoza was a 17th century Jewish-Dutch philosopher).

It is here that I wish to thank Olive Ray and Robin Evans of The Lowestoft Spiritual Centre, Gt. Yarmouth, G.B., who have been gracious in their advice and in allowing the use of material pertinent to their Centre. I thank you for reading this book and sincerely hope it helps to expand mankind's limited knowledge into the unknown.

---

7   Nautlis. Einstein Reconciliating Religion and Science. http://nautil.us/blog/how-einstein-reconciled-religion-to-science Accessed 22/11/2020.

Made in the USA
Las Vegas, NV
22 August 2021